SUCCESSFUL CONSULTANT TRAINING

presents

Consultant in a Book

Unlock Your Potential
& Basic Training
Manual

SUCCESSFUL CONSULTANT TRAINING
Consultant in a Book

Successful Consultant Training
274 Craftsbury Road
Greensboro, VT 05841
info@successfulconsultanttraining.com
http://successfulconsultanttraining.com

April 2013

Note to Readers

This book is intended as a source of informative material to those people who are interested in becoming a consultant, or freelancer, or for existing consultants who want to improve their results.

This book may not be suitable for everyone, and does not promise or guarantee of results or earnings. Your earnings potential is entirely up to you and the actions you decide to take. Although this book was written in good faith, the contents may include inaccuracies or typographical errors.

The author and publisher are not providing legal, financial, or accounting services. The reader should consult a professional in these fields before implementing any suggestions made in this book. The author and publisher disclaim any responsibility for any liability or loss, which occurred as a direct result of using the material contained in this book.

Table of Contents

Consultant in a Book Introduction

Your trainer: Dan Predpall, Founder & President of Successful Consultant Training

Welcome to your Consultant-in-a-Book training! The material in this book includes best practices I've applied during a consulting career spanning 35 years and counting, in addition to some of the latest and greatest business techniques being used today.

This book was written for individuals who want to monetize their knowledge and skills. Most people, through their life experiences (work, hobbies, interests, school, etc.), have accumulated information that other people want to know about. More importantly, many people want to work on their own, want to become an independent consultant. Of course, practicing consultants also will benefit from this book.

The market for independent consultants, freelancers, and contractors has never been better. Firms are reticent to hire full-time employees these days because of the slow economy. The overhead cost of hiring employees has risen significantly in recent years, making it advantageous for firms to engage consultants as long as they can before hiring.

The Internet is providing unprecedented access to massive amounts of data and information that can be useful to consultants. We are in a digital age, where the cost for equipment needed to operate a successful has never been lower, and is not a barrier to starting a consultancy. And, you can outsource tasks you need quickly and at low rates through online sites like Elance or Vworker.

More importantly, we are in a marketing revolution. Through sites such as Facebook, LinkedIn, Google Plus, Yahoo, and Youtube, you have access to literally a billion potential customers worldwide! And, the cost is minimal. Furthermore, marketing is largely education-based today, so if you can tell prospects about your offering, you can succeed.

In addition, the lifestyle gained by self-employment can be quite attractive. You have exceptional flexibility with regard to working hours. You control whom you work for. You decide how much you want to earn (obviously a function of how many hours you choose to work and the particular markets you pursue). Because of the technology available, and the Internet, you can live in virtually any location you choose, as long as long as you can get DSL or some other high-speed access to the Internet.

I use the term "consultant" because I've worked in consulting for most of the last 35 years of my career. However, don't let this term hold you back. Thousands of individuals every year start their own businesses and sell advice, training, or other services for a fee.

Consultant's Success Parthenon

The Consultant-in-a-Book covers what I call the four pillars of consulting: Your Offering, Business Development (markets), Client Service (customers), and

Problem Solving (perform your services). However, your success with these pillars will depend upon your mindset. Once you learn the pillars, you are ready to start your consulting business by creating a business plan. The business plan becomes the foundation for a successful enterprise. And, once again, if you are a practicing consultant, on your own or working in a firm, the concepts, methods and techniques covered here will help you improve your results.

The four pillars of consulting are universal; they apply to any business that utilizes both people and information—in other words, almost every business you can imagine. If you learn the four pillars (along with the proper mindset and business plan), you will be prepared to embark on an exciting new business of your choice, or improve and expand the business you have.

We begin with a chapter on mindset. I believe strongly that to be an effective consultant, you must have a "consultant's mindset." Over the several decades I've been consulting, I developed "the Consultant's Cycle of Success," the seven essential success factors in the consultant's mindset. We will cover them in Chapter 1.

Next we will move to the first pillar, Your Offering. Obviously, you will offer some type of service. So, before we get into the skills consultants must have, we dive into the service you want to offer. I learned a long time ago that success in consulting is a direct function of how well you understand the service you are offering. I know that on the surface, this sounds strange. Trust me on this for now.

The second pillar is Business Development, or alternatively, marketing and sales. Marketing is probably the most important skill a consultant can have. Without it, you won't have many chances to perform your service! On the other hand, if you really master business development, your success will be unlimited. We cover a multitude of marketing and sales techniques that will help you find more business leads, and help you convert more of those leads into revenues.

The third pillar is Problem Solving. Most consultants or freelancers solve problems. Companies hire consultants to solve problems. So, if you have strong problem-solving skills, you will make a good impression with your customers. However, few consultants have been taught problem solving. We'll get you started here.

The fourth pillar is Client Development. Most of your revenue in the long term will come from repeat business. You must make every effort to satisfy—no, delight, your customers, so they come back for more. We will show you how to keep those clients happy.

Then we finish with Business Planning. I've never met a consultant who likes planning. Most people look at planning as boring and a time waster. However, the most successful consultants are perennial planners! We'll present a process to create a business plan that will help you to "plan for success".

You are about to embark on an exciting journey that will surely lead to greater success in your existing business, or will show you how to "get off on the right foot" in your new business. The techniques presented in this book have worked well for me throughout a long career in consulting. They will work for you, too.

We are here to support you. You will have questions about the material. Just email us at <u>info@successfulconsultant-training.com</u> and we will get back to you. Better yet, post a comment on our Facebook page:

https://www.facebook.com/SuccessfulConsultantTraining

Your Success Roadmap

At the end of this book you will see a chapter called, "Your Roadmap to Success". The roadmap chapter provides a series of activities to complete as you read this book. These activities take you through the four pillars of consulting in addition to Mindset and Business Planning.

I will ask you to perform a number of activities that will apply to you if you are just starting out and you want to become a consultant, or if you are an existing consultant or business owner. If you're just starting out, you will create your first Roadmap. If you are a practicing consultant, your purpose will be to review where you are, and improve upon each of the activities. If you have never addressed some of the activities, do it now.

Performing these exercises is very important if you are here to learn. We learn in one of two ways: through self-discovery (often influenced by coaching or mentoring), or implementing a technique we were shown (your assignment here).

Purchase a hardbound or spiral-bound notebook. Create "chapters" that correspond to the sections in the Roadmap:

1. Define Your Business Objective

2. Reverse Engineer the Objective

3. Set Your Goals

4. Specify Your Action Items

5. Mind Your Mindset!

6. What is Your Offering?

7. Prepare Your Marketing Plan

8. Develop Your Sales Plan

9. Develop Your Proposal Template

10. Develop Your Problem Assessment Technique

11. How Will You Select the Best Solution?

12. What is Your Client Relationship Plan?

13. Prepare Your Project Management Plan

14. Prepare Your Business Plan & Get Started!

As you proceed through this training, I will direct you to perform the exercises discussed in each chapter.

If you are serious about making money as a consultant or freelancer, or any business for that matter, just reading this book likely won't be enough. As I mentioned earlier, learning requires more effort than simply reading a book. That's why we've included the Success Roadmap. If you perform the exercises in the fourteen sections of the Roadmap, you will practice what you've learned. Even better, you will end up with a specific plan for you to start your consulting business!

If you are interested in learning more about the techniques presented here, at the end of this book we describe some available support materials.

1. The Consultant's Mindset

One of the first things I learned from my mentor, Prof. W. Edwards Deming, was the importance of mindset. He constantly stressed that success comes from being motivated from inside–or, as he stated it, by intrinsic motivation. In other words, it is your responsibility to establish a mindset that drives you forward. You will not get that mindset from anywhere else (e.g., extrinsic motivation).

As I continued my consulting career, I became more and more aware of the behaviors that seemed to spur me on, or that helped my employees be more productive and energized. I concluded that seven essential factors largely govern success in consulting. They are: vision, goal setting, enthusiasm, focus, creativity, teamship, and mastery. I call these behaviors "the Consultant's Cycle of Success".

1. Develop a Vision
6. Build Teams
5. Be Creative
7. Mastery
2. Set Goals
4. Maintain Focus
3. Display Enthusiasm

Let's take a brief look at each of these seven behaviors, and how they relate to your success.

Vision

We are talking about your personal vision here. A personal

> *"You can't perform in a manner that is inconsistent with the way you see yourself."*
>
> **Dr. Joyce Brothers**

vision is how you wish to build your future or design your life, and the environment around it. A clear vision is very empowering. Your vision should be based upon your values. For example, four of my values are "owning my own business", "living near a beautiful lake", "learning fast", and "improving the lives of others."

Your vision must be positive. Many people have negative visions, such as "I want to get rid of that boring job". That vision, of course, isn't empowering!

The importance of having a personal vision was never stated better than the words of Napoleon Hill: "The psychological effect of having a personal vision is to impress the vision upon your subconscious mind so strongly that it accepts that purpose as a pattern or blueprint that will eventually dominate your actions." Think about this quote for a minute. I think it is profound (and true!).

Conversely, if you don't think about your own vision, you will live the visions of others, and you will live out someone else's dream. That is not a pleasant thought! Take a couple of hours and create your vision now! Know that there is no wrong way to approach this, and that you will be able to refine or revise your vision as you move forward in your career.

For example, here is my vision: "To continually develop my potential by keeping a focus on my business, my family, and my health goals. Strive to improve the lives of others through education and innovation."

The next step in your "visioning" is to develop a "business objective", or vision of where you would like to see your business in 2 or 3 years, whether you are just starting your

---

"Never go to sleep without a request to your subconscious."
—*Thomas Edison*

---

consulting business, or seeking to improve your existing business. Establishing a business objective helps you determine the level of effort needed to meet your objective. This is a critical planning step.

Now it is time to start your Success Roadmap. Go to Chapter 7 and complete sections 1 and 2 in the Roadmap (business objective and reverse engineer your objective).

Goal Setting

Based on my experience, goal setting is one of the most important activities a consultant can do. Why? Most consultants work independently, whether they work in a consulting firm or on their own. In order to reach their potential, they need a target. Lily Tomlin said it well: "I wanted to be someone. I guess I should have been more specific." Brian Tracy was even more direct: "Working without goals is like driving in a fog."

Goals have been called "a dream with a deadline" and "a contract with yourself". So, why don't most people set goals for themselves? The most common answer is that they don't believe goals will make a difference. But goals can make all the difference in the world—the difference between daydreams and reality.

Why do goals work? Goals focus you more on long-term activities that will really make a difference, as opposed to the short-term activities like answering emails, watching TV, and addressing your latest crisis.

But the most important contribution of goal setting, in my opinion, is that it connects your conscious mind with your subconscious mind. The "real work" is accomplished by the subconscious mind. Our subconscious mind is not self-directed. It only reacts to what we pay attention to. Most of us never "program" this part of our brain, which is also the most powerful part. By setting goals consistent with our vision and values, and reading them frequently, we tell our subconscious what is important to us. If you don't provide a direction to your subconscious, your "old programs" will continue, bringing you the same results you've gotten.

To close this discussion of goals, I would like to show you a quote that was written almost 3,000 years ago by the ancient Vedic Upanishads:

You are what your deepest desire is.

As is your desire, so is your intention.

As is your intention, so is your will.

As is your will, so is your deed.

As is your deed, so is your destiny.

How do you set goals? The SMART acronym has been around for years:

▶ **S**: Make goals very **specific**. If you want to improve at baseball, make one goal associated with your batting average.

▶ **M**: Goals should be **measurable**. "I will keep my batting average above 300".

▶ **A**: Make goals **attainable**. That doesn't mean easily attainable, but rather a "stretch goal" that challenges you.

▶ **R**: Make your goals **relevant**. That means the goal must be consistent with your vision or overall objectives. In other words, there must be a reason for the goal.

▶ **T**: Goals must be tied to a **time** period. In other words, there must be a deadline for every goal.

Here's one more tip. Goals should be broken down into weekly and monthly chunks to be effective. Also, try reading your goals

every morning. That will keep your goals active in your conscious and subconscious mind.

Now go Chapter 7, the Success Roadmap, Section 3, and set some goals for yourself, goals that inspire you and that you truly want, and you will notice

the difference!

Then proceed to Section 4 of the Success Roadmap, where you will be asked to create more specific actions from your goals.

Enthusiasm

Once again, I will let others speak for me regarding the value of enthusiasm. Napoleon Hill stated: "Enthusiasm is a state of mind that inspires and arouses one to put action into the task at hand." Still not convinced? "Enthusiasm is energizing, like electricity. Without it you will be like a dead battery." Yours truly.

The only point I am making here is that if you want to be successful, really successful, and enjoy the benefits of that success, you must be passionate about your work. When you care about what you do, you become more energetic and enthusiastic. It is as simple as that. When you are enthusiastic, something amazing happens: you produce results, not excuses.

Focus

Once again, I will let others speak first. Tony Robbins says it best about focus: "One reason so few of us achieve what we truly want is that we never direct our focus; we never concentrate our power. Most people dabble their way through life, never deciding to master anything in particular."

There are two dimensions to focus. The first, directing, was mentioned by Robbins. Many people never direct their focus on their vision. As a result, their results are disappointing, never reaching a point where their lifestyle is improved. The second dimension is too many "foci". I've seen many people pursue three or four jobs at once, and wind up unable to dedicate sufficient effort to succeed at any.

Here is an interesting story about focus. A golfer comes to within 100 yards of a green. The green has a pond to the left and a large sand trap on the right of the green. The average golfer will have a conversation in his/her mind that goes something like this: "don't hit the ball into the water or into the trap." A good golfer will aim directly at the pin and ignore the trap and water. That is the power of focus. In general, most of us focus on why we can't meet a goal, rather than how we will.

Focusing on a vision or goal activates your pattern recognition system. Our brain works by searching for patterns. For example, if you just bought a red car, you will start seeing red cars all over the road. Why? The fact that you spent so much money on your red car was a message to your brain that red cars are important. Your brain starts finding red cars for you!

In summary, focus on what is important. Eliminate distractions. Concentrate your focus like a rifle shot, not a shotgun shot.

Creativity

Creativity leads to innovation, and innovative consultants always win. So, it is vital that we consultants be creative. There are two forms of creativity: personal and collaborative.

It is an interesting fact that most people do not set aside time to be creative. I am not sure why, but busy lives probably has something to do with it. To be creative, we must "do it". We must set aside time for creativity and innovation. We must do our creative work in a quiet place, without music, without people, and without TV. Personal creativity is just that: personal.

Your personal creative juices can be activated by setting goals like, "I need a new service to offer to my clients." By the way, the more optimistic you are, *the more creative you will be.*

The second form of creativity is collaborative. The essence of collaborative creativity is leveraging your relationships. You put the word out that you need help creating. Ask for help. Ask for advice. Ask for information, suggestions, or ideas. Brainstorm with others. The old adage "two heads are better than one" is still true today!

Set aside time for creativity. Set goals for yourself to create better marketing systems and improved services or products, and, of course, new services.

Teamship

Jay Abraham once said, "Employing the collaborative help of others is crucial to success." In other words, you can't do it all yourself. You aren't smart enough, and you don't have the time to do it alone. Teamship means working together as a team. Reach out to others for help and advice.

> *If I could solve all the problems myself, I would.*
>
> **Thomas Edison, when asked why he had a team of twenty-one assistants**

Teamship also includes getting support from mentors, coaches, or other reference groups that can bring new thinking and behaviors, so crucial to moving your results to a higher level.

Another aspect of teamship is learning how to facilitate teams or groups. As consultants, we often lead teams comprising staff from our client firms. Good facilitation skills equate to good leadership skills. Always begin meetings with a review of the agenda (never hold a meeting without one). Take copious notes, or appoint a recorder to take notes. Putting notes onto flip chart paper, and hanging them on a wall as I proceed, has been a very helpful tool for me over the years. Finally, I always end a meeting with action plans and work assignments.

Isaac Newton understood the importance of teamship: "If I have seen further than others, it is by standing upon the shoulders of giants."

Mastery

The seventh and last factor is mastery. This factor is taken directly from Dr. Deming's philosophy of continuous improvement. First, to achieve mastery, you must focus on your intrinsic desires (e.g. "helping others"). You achieve that desire by learning, or expanding your ability to create the results you want. Second, if you devote effort to improving your expertise and your service over the years, that effort will certainly lead to mastery.

Continuous improvement also means repetition. The best way to engage your subconscious is repetition, which creates new neural pathways in your brain. Repetition leads to mastery.

I am an excellent example. I learned how to find sites for new power generation facilities early in my consulting career. I enjoyed this work, and as I performed each study I tried to improve over the last study. After performing one hundred or more of these studies, I rose to become a national leader in this field. Continuous improvement works!

To this day, I continue to monitor my performance against these seven behaviors. Together, they form a powerful force that propels you forward. Once again, a number of these behaviors originated from Prof. Deming's teachings.

Before moving on, I want to mention the work of Stanford University psychologist, Dr. Carol Dweck. She conducted some remarkable research on mindset, from the perspective of growth versus non-growth. Her research provides a great source of insight into the mindset of someone who is motivated for success. She also clearly defined the elements of a growth mindset.

For example, in a growth mindset, hard work is respected, and leads to mastery, as we just noted, whereas in a non-growth environment, hard work is devalued ("why work when I already know everything?").

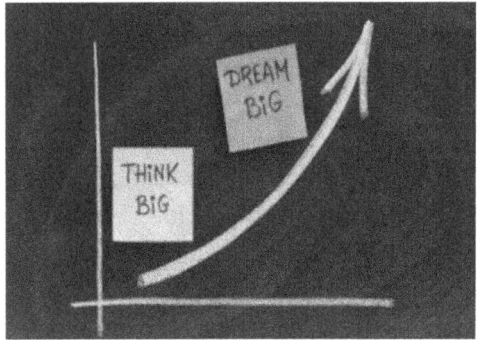

People with a growth mindset understand that success comes after consistent and persistent hard work, whereas the non-growth people want instant gratification.

Individuals with a growth mindset use criticism to improve, while the non-growth individuals look at criticism as a personal attack.

Growth-minded people get inspiration from the success of others, whereas non-growth-minded people merely envy successful individuals ("I deserve what they have").

Can you see the difference between the growth and non-growth mindsets? The difference is stark. Try creating a short table with two columns. Call the left column "growth mindset" and the right, "non-growth mindset". Describe growth mindset examples with a short phrase (e.g., values hard work), and describe the non-growth mindset directly across in the right column (e.g., devalues hard work).

Put that table on your office wall.

Now complete Section 4, Specify Your Action Items, in your Success Roadmap, Chapter 7. Go ahead and complete Section 5, Mind Your Mindset, too!

Once you've completed these sections in the Roadmap to Success chapter, proceed to Chapter 2, below.

As we mentioned above, you will learn this material only if you implement it, not if you just read it.

2. Define Your Offering

We will start by defining your offering, although we will use a few steps to get there. Everything must begin with your offering. You must have a complete understanding of your offering because it affects so many other aspects of your business, such as marketing, client expectations, and project management. If you don't have a detailed understanding of your offering, how can you expect to be able to describe it, in detail, to your prospective clients?

What Is Your Income Goal?

OK, now you're thinking, what does my income goal have to do with my offering? Good question. We just mentioned that understanding your offering is connected to many other parts of your business. Well, your offering is connected to your income goal! Here's why. Suppose you want to sell a $7 e-book on interior decorating. Your estimate of sales in the first year is 5,000 e-books. Assume that you needed $70,000 to properly support your family in the next year. Well, your offering of a $7 e-book will only get you to $35,000; it won't meet your income goal. This will force you to alter your offering, perhaps making a bigger, more detailed $29 e-book instead, or changing your marketing plan in order to increase your sales. You get the idea.

Let's determine your income goal. First, list your personal and family expenses per month (things like rent, car payments, health insurance, food, gasoline, maintenance, phone, entertainment, clothing, and savings). Next, list your monthly business expenses (such as office rent, communications, legal support, administrative or other professional assistance, business insurance, computers, stationary and other office supplies, travel and related costs, and bank loans).

Now add up the expenses, then include a contingency (usually 5%), and add the estimated tax bill (for simplicity, use 20%). That dollar amount should approximate your income goal for the next year. Keep that number in mind as we move forward.

What Is Your Topic and Expertise?

If you are just starting out and want to become a consultant, help people solve problems, or give advice and monetize your knowledge, what is the topic you have chosen? Most people will use the knowledge or skills they have gained from their work experience, or from their hobby or area of interest. However, many people pick topics in which they have a high level of enthusiasm and interest, and then study this topic. With the information available on the Internet, anyone can become an expert in a field quickly (often in a matter of weeks).

To be successful with your offering, you must be enthusiastic about it. As Napoleon Hill said, "Enthusiasm is a state of mind that inspires and arouses one to put action into the task at hand". Enthusiasm will be your drive. Make sure you have it.

Your expertise is what you will be known for. It forms the foundation for your offering. Your position as an expert will engender trust and credibility. If you think that your expertise is solid, let's move forward. On the other hand, if you need to strengthen your knowledge, do so. The effort will pay off.

Now, before we talk about your offering, we need to understand your audience.

Who Is Your Audience?

Who will you sell your service to? Will you sell to businesses? Will you sell to consumers? Even if you are selling to businesses, remember that businesses are run by people. You need to understand the profile of a potential customer (your audience).

Create an "ideal profile" of your audience. What is their age? Are they mostly men or women? Do they hail from a geographic area or country? What are their interests? What is their cultural background? What careers do they pursue? Are they typically single or married? How many children do they have? What is the level of their education?

Now look at their emotional situation. What frustrates them? What worries them? What do they want more of? What are their aspirations? What are their goals? We are looking for the buying motives of your prospects.

For example, I sell to engineers and scientists. From my experience, this group is quite comfortable with data. They like to draw their own conclusions about the data. This group responds well to authority because most engineers and scientists work in a hierarchical business environment. Also, this group responds to standards, which are prevalent in their fields. Therefore, it helps to describe your service as a standard. These are a few examples of how buying motives help you sell.

It is natural if you are having trouble understanding buying motives. The Internet can help you research either business professionals or consumers, if you don't already know your audience well. For example, LinkedIn may be of help. Of course, the best solution is to interview a few prospects!

What Is Your Customer's Key Problem?

OK, now that you have profiles of your audience, you must develop a good understanding of their problem. When a customer has a problem, they are motivated to solve the problem.

In addition, if you show them that you understand their problem, you have increased their confidence in you. Customers buy confidence. They want to know that when they buy from you, the problem will go away. For sure.

So, look at your customer's problem. Create a description of that problem that is more precise than your customer's. Make sure that the problem isn't just a symptom. What is the underlying problem? For example, if you are a marketing consultant, and you just took on a client who has too few customers to support his business, the symptom is "not enough clients". The problem likely is a poorly executed marketing process. The cure might be to create an effective marketing plan.

Another example: you are a consultant, and you receive a Request for Proposal from a town to design a new hiking and biking trail. What is the problem? Designing a hiking and biking trail? No. The problem is getting the Town Council to approve the trail. I can't overestimate the value of distinguishing the symptoms from the problems; this skill is at the heart of your potential for success as a consultant, regardless of the field you choose.

How do we determine the customer's problem? There are two ways:

1. **Go to the source**. This is the best way to determine customer needs. For example, you can conduct a survey on the Internet, or by phone. Or, you can call a few prospects. Another idea is to offer a free service in return for asking them about their needs and wants.

2. **Do some research**. You can find tons of information about the business that your customer is in. For example, we just completed some market research for one of my consulting companies that works in power plant site selection. We reviewed trade association newsletters and set Google alerts in several topics. We found that many coal plants were shutting down in the eastern U.S. due to stricter Environmental Protection Agency emission standards. This will create the need for many more natural-gas power plant projects.

What Is Your Offering?

OK, now let's go to your service or product offering. Your offering must be congruent with your audience's needs. If you accomplish this, I call it your "magic formula". Most consultants sell their product or service. They talk a lot about how great it is. They talk about how great they are, too. And, they talk about how great their business is.

Well, that is fine, but that isn't what the audience (your customer) wants to hear. *Rather, they want to know what your service will do for them.* In other words, most consultants talk a lot about the features of their product, but they don't say enough about the benefits of the product for the customer.

When there is a perfect match between your product and your audience, you don't have to convince them to buy. They become pre-sold. Prospects will see the value in your product and they will buy. *If you offer great content, and it benefits the prospect, you will not need to sell anything.*

OK, it's time to see if you really understand your offer, and if it will have "customer appeal".

Can you answer the following questions about your offer?

1. **What is your offering called?** Does it have a catchy name? If you owned a Motel in Albany, do you call it "Albany Motel", or something like "Do Drop Inn"?

2. **What is the offering?** If you were an investment counselor, you might say, "I develop investment plans to grow retirees' nest eggs".

3. **What does your offering do?** The investment counselor might say, "I allocate funds to an array of investment vehicles so as to maximize return".

4. **How does it work?** The investment counselor might say he considers stocks, bonds, Exchange Traded Funds (ETFs), Exchange Traded Notes (ETNs) and commodities, and selects the investments with the highest return and acceptable risk.

5. **What are the benefits for the customer?** Benefits must include both the benefits for the customer's firm as well as benefits for your direct contact. Firm benefits are more rational, while your contact benefits will be based more on emotion.

6. **How is the product or service different from competitor versions?** What have you done to make your product more attractive to customers and different versus your competition?

7. **What is the value of your service, in dollars, to your customer?** What is it worth to them? Does your service increase profitability? Does it save time? Increase product quality or accuracy? Express the value of your service in your customer's terms.

8. **What is the price for your service or product?** How do you put the price in a perspective that makes the price appear attractive? Can you compare the price to the value? Will it save money for the customer? How much?

9. **What is your guarantee?** It is important to express a guarantee because it reduces the risk to the buyer.

If you don't have a specific money-back guarantee, what other ways can you reduce purchase risk?

10. **What social proof do you have that demonstrates experience with your service?** Do you have endorsements or testimonials? Letters of recommendation? Completed examples of your work that would impress your potential client?

If you can answer these questions about your offering, that's great and you're way ahead in the game. If you can't, start jotting down notes about how you might answer these questions.

What Is the Marketability of Your Offering?

Lastly, you must determine if there is a market for your service. Can you sell enough of the service to meet your income goal? You can answer this question by conducting some market research.

Market research is carried out in two ways: direct and indirect.

1. Direct research is first hand, communicating directly with the prospects via phone, email or mail surveys. This is the best, and more reliable research.

2. Indirect methods include data collected by others, such as market research reports, government publications, university studies, or studies promoted by trade associations.

Two online sources that may help are Clickbank and Amazon. These sites sell thousands of products, including information products, consulting, and physical products.

Another excellent source of market data are market research reports prepared by research firms. For example, if you Google "market research for interior design", you will find reports that provide the following information about this field:

- ▶ Sales volume and trends
- ▶ Employment data
- ▶ Industry sectors and subsectors
- ▶ Five-year business trends
- ▶ Residential versus commercial establishments

Finally, try using Google searches, or use the Google Keyword tool. Another idea, try www.similarsitesearch. com Use this tool to identify and learn about your competition.

The bottom line is that you want to be certain that there is a market out there for your product, and that you know who your target audience is.

OK, now proceed to Your Success Roadmap (Chapter 7) and complete Section 6, Your Offering. Then begin Chapter 3 below.

3. Business Development for Consultants

I f you asked 100 consultants and aspiring consultants what their biggest worry is, 90% of the responses would be getting enough business to meet their goals, whether a revenue goal if they work in a firm, or a profit goal if they are independent consultants.

That's why we're going to spend so much time on this topic. We will start with the basics and move to more advanced topics that will appeal to everyone.

Let's start with some definitions. Look at the "business development spectrum". We begin business development with marketing and we end with sales (and wins!). Of course, the dividing line between marketing and sales is somewhat blurred.

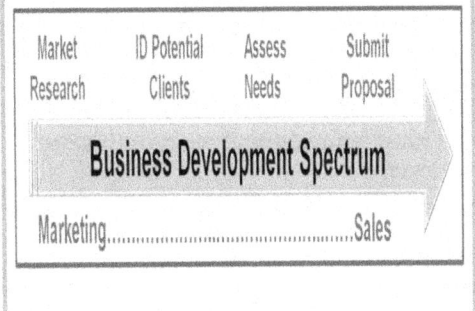

The first step is market research, with a purpose of identifying the markets that will be attractive for you and learning about those markets. The market research should lead to identification of prospects that will appreciate and, hopefully purchase, your service. Then you assess the specific needs, wants, and desires of your prospects and refine your service offerings accordingly. Firmly in sales territory, you receive opportunities to bid on projects, or, better still, clients engage you outright!

Marketing includes:

► identifying your target markets,
► understanding buyer motives,
► developing marketing materials, and
► identifying prospects.

Selling includes:

► building relationships with prospects,
► understanding buyer needs, and
► addressing buyer objections.

With that introduction, let's move to market psychology.

Market Psychology

The study of marketing psychology has been around for a century, and is an absolute requirement for successful marketing. However, I don't think a lot of consultants recognize the role psychology plays in their business success.

Edward Bernays (1891-1995) was a pioneer in public relations and crowd psychology. His uncle was Sigmund Freud. His seminal book was called "Propaganda", in which is taught the concept of "opinion-molding", a technique used to this day by politicians. He argued that public opinion must be manipulated through understanding of the mental processes of the masses. He invented the "press release" and the "bacon and eggs breakfast"... yes, he was the first to put bacon and eggs together (at least for sale to the public!)… he did it in an advertisement for a restaurant.

Bernays' contribution to marketing was his statement, "emotion wins over the heart; logic wins over the mind". We employ this concept by appealing to the prospect's emotional needs first, followed by a logical presentation of why he should purchase your service or product.

This point is so important that I quote one of the most successful marketers, Joe Sugerman: "It is estimated that 95% of the reasons a prospect buys involve a subconscious decision." Think about this for at least 60 seconds. Seriously. What does this statement mean with regard to how you market your services?

This quote becomes even more interesting when we listen to Jonah Lehrer, author of *How We Decide*. He says that

---

"The crucial importance of our emotions is the fact that we can't make decisions without them. The emotional brain is especially useful at helping us make hard decisions."
—Jonah Lehrer

---

our brain is built in such a way that all decisions are made with a significant contribution by our "emotional brain".

Is the importance of these concepts sinking in? We want to take advantage of the emotional brain's role in making buying decisions. One way we do this is through influence. How can we influence our prospect to buy? (I want to add a sidebar here. The fact that we have to talk in clinical terms doesn't mean we're trying to manipulate

"I never discovered anything with my rational brain."

Albert Einstein

our potential clients—at least, not to their detriment. If you're offering a good product or service that you stand behind, then you're *helping every client succeed*. If you're offering a product or service that your client needs, then knowing how best to present your offering and gain your clients' confidence is a "win" for both of you.)

Influencers

Our job as a consultant selling a service is to motivate the prospect to take action and buy. Motivation is energized by emotion. Emotions trigger a response to a feeling. That feeling may be a need that is awakened or recognized. So, we must ensure that the prospect sees the emotional benefits of the service or offering. One way to accomplish this is through the use of "influencers".

If we use emotional influencers, we call them "intrinsic motivators". If we use facts or logic to influence, we call them "extrinsic motivators". Clearly, we put a much higher priority on intrinsic influence. There are quite a number of influencers. The more you can include in a marketing or sales piece, the better. Let's look at a few influencers.

▶ Reciprocity: Robert Cialdini, in his book *Influence*, says that "reciprocation possesses awesome strength, often producing a 'yes' response to a request that, except for the feeling of indebtedness, would have surely been refused." One of the most powerful uses of reciprocation is giving "free stuff". This can be a free report, a free audit, a free evaluation of some kind, a free newsletter, or free training. The point is that your prospect or client will want to return the favor. Use free stuff to get appointments, get an opportunity to propose, or be considered more seriously in a competition. Make sure what you're giving them is something they want. We've all received a pen with a company's name on it; giving them something that solves a problem for them is much more influential.

▶ Social Proof: Buyers always like to know that other people purchased your product and thought it was useful. The most common way to show social proof is testimonials, which can be shown as a video, an audio recording, or in written form. If you are just starting out, and you don't have any testimonials, talk about your own accomplishments (i.e., authority).

▶ Your Mirror Image: Here's one you may not have thought about. This is a very powerful influencer. First, characterize yourself. Who are you? What are your interests? Your education? Your age? Your values? Music lover versus art lover? Then search out prospects who have a similar "identity". You will be more successful selling to these prospects than anyone else. Why? Because they are just like you.

▶ Urgency and Scarcity: Both of these influencers are terrific. If a situation is urgent, it compels the prospect to action. If the product is scarce, a

prospect feels the impulse to buy. When you see products sold on the Internet, the seller always says something like "only 20 left" or "this sale shuts down in 24 hours". Think about why auctions are so popular. They involve both influencers!

▶ Authority: Prospects and clients like to buy from someone with authority. What does this really mean? It could be a title, such as President, or Professor. Or, you may be a recognized expert in your field; this commands authority. Your advanced education works, too (Dr.). When giving a presentation to a client, always have someone with "authority" lead off the session.

▶ Differentiation/Comparison/Contrast: This influencer is used to set your service apart from your competition. Do that by indicating that your service performs the required task faster, better, or cheaper. Or, compare your product with another one that is inferior. Contrast is a powerful technique as well. When someone buys a $300 product, they are often upsold with a series of products that are lower in cost. By showing the contrast, buyers see the lower costs of the upsells as *much lower*, and are more likely to buy. (Think about a Nintendo Wii vs. the cost of the game packages—or fries with that burger!)

▶ Leading Edge: People love to purchase the latest new thing. When you are marketing your service, always indicate what latest and greatest techniques you are using, or the latest technology. People prefer to buy from leaders.

> *"Success means never letting the competition define you. Instead you have to define yourself based on a point of view you care deeply about."*
>
> *—Tom Chappell, Tom's Of Maine*

▶ Justification of Value: Prospects and clients always want to know that they are getting a good deal. When you mention a price for a product or service, the prospect immediately starts a mental exercise where they compare your product with others, in terms of value and price. Well, don't let them do these mental machinations in their head. Do it for them! One way is to show a replacement value. Another is to indicate a result higher than the cost. For example, if you are selling a marketing course, show that the buyer will win two more jobs in the next three months, which equals several times the cost of the course.

Once again, use as many of these influencers as possible in your sales message.

Foundational Marketing and Sales Techniques

Let's consider the key marketing and sales concepts and techniques. I believe these eight techniques are 'essential' to a solid and successful marketing effort:

> ▶ **A Campaign versus an Event**: Marketing is a continuous process. Put another way, marketing is like a campaign, not an event. There is an old adage that it takes seven contacts with a prospect to get your first response (let alone your first sale!). Therefore, you need to plan out the ways you will contact each prospect. Start with an email, perhaps, and follow up with another email, a hard copy letter, a free audio or video, another email, and a phone call.

> ▶ **Marketing Channels**: When we say marketing channels, we mean the methods you use to reach your prospects and clients. Most consultants tend to use one channel that they are most comfortable with. The problem with that strategy is that not all prospects will respond to one channel. Your marketing message will vary with the channel, and the universe of prospects can be quite different

by channel. Examples of marketing channels are: direct response marketing (includes direct mail); Internet marketing via Facebook, LinkedIn, or Google; radio; TV; press releases; referrals; and, of course, "cold calls" to potentially attractive prospects within your market sub-sector.

▶ **Educate versus Sell**: I think Jeff Gitomer says it best: "When you sell, you break rapport; when you educate you build it". In other words, what would you rather do: try to convince a prospect to purchase your service or product, or educate the prospect about your offering so the prospect *decides* to buy? What do you think your prospect would prefer? Another way to explain this approach is that through education, you essentially pre-sell your service.

There are many advantages to educating your client. Perhaps the biggest benefit is that by educating, you position yourself as the expert, which increases your credibility. Also, by educating, you can demonstrate that your service is better than the competition.

If you are still not convinced, consider this classic example of education: Schlitz beer. This brand was virtually unknown until they began telling people that they used pure water from artesian wells, a three-loop distillation process, steamed their bottles for cleanliness, and so on. All other breweries did the same thing. However, by educating the consumer, they rocketed to #8 in sales within six months.

Finally, Jay Abraham says this about educating your client: "Your prospects won't understand or appreciate a value, or a service, or a benefit, unless or until you educate them to appreciate it".

If you like beer you'll *love* Schlitz

▶ **Build your Network**: All successful consultants have built valuable networks. You build a network by getting involved. Determine where your prospects gather (trade association meetings, conferences, Chamber of Commerce breakfast meetings, professional association meetings, local civil groups, and blogs or forums on the Internet). The most effective thing you can do is present papers at these meetings, or contribute good ideas on the blogs. This will help establish you as an expert.

▶ **Provide Exceptional Value**: if you don't provide your client with exceptional value, all of your marketing won't accomplish its goal. And, it isn't sufficient to have great content. Your offering must be related to the needs and wants of your target market.

> *"Try not to become a man of success, but rather a man of value."*
>
> Albert Einstein

Be sure you understand your audience and what they expect from you. Then customize your offering to that expectation. Value can equate to a unique tool or software, or approach to solving a problem. Value can mean faster, less expensive, higher in quality, cutting edge, or more comprehensive.

Exceptional value, then, means both great content as well as a very close match to your prospect's needs.

▶ **Compelling Sales Message**: We just mentioned how important it is to have great content. It is also important to craft a compelling sales message. So, just what is a compelling marketing message? It is a clearly described benefit, exceptional value, or powerful result you offer that makes your services profoundly more attractive than your competition with regard to fulfilling the needs of your client. Yes, it is a bit of a mouthful... yet it is concise.

Now, your sales message can be written from one of three perspectives: yours, your competitor's, or your customer's. A sales message written from your own perspective will be weak. A sales message written from the perspective of your competition is better, but still weak. You must write your sales message from your customer's perspective.

The best way to accomplish this is to determine the two benefits that your customer thinks are most important to him/her. Write your sales message around them.

You're not finished. Now show the customer some "proof" that your message works. The best way to do this is through a testimonial. However, a case history will work, too. Concisely describe a case where a customer used your service and gained exceptional value.

Here is an example of a good sales message: "Every independent consultant needs to keep track of the numbers. The problem is, you hate to do this, and you don't want to pay to outsource it. We build custom, easy-to-use software solutions that will perform virtually all of this work for you... in house, fast, and affordable."

Another example: "We use the latest technology and plantings to protect your home from weather damage while creating a landscape that will give your home a unique appeal, all at competitive prices."

▶ **Benefits versus Features**: We can identify four levels of service benefits:

- covert benefits,
- overt benefits,
- advantages, and
- features.

It is important to understand the differences.

Covert benefits are those benefits that appeal to the emotions of the customer. Examples might include soft issues such as status, or perks. Or, it could mean saving time or money, or providing security. The key issue here is that covert benefits appeal directly to a person, not a firm. What do they want from your service?

Overt benefits include, for example, a lower-cost solution, a technically superior solution, or better schedule. Overt benefits relate more to the customer's firm.

Advantages address how your service is better than the competition. Examples could be that your office is closer to the customer than your competitor's office, or your project manager will reside in the customer's office for the duration of the project to improve communication. These advantages are directed at your competition.

Finally, **features** will include the number of staff you have, how long you have been in business, or that you have your own field instruments or other specialized equipment so you don't have to lease them. Features are the weakest form of reasons why a customer should buy from you.

> ► **Minimize Purchase Risk**: When you are trying to get the first sale from a prospect, they will have trepidation about buying from you. It is natural. They don't know you yet. You must offer something to make buying from you less risky. Fortunately, there are a number of ways to do this.
>
> The obvious way is to offer a solid guarantee, such as a money back guarantee. Many consultants shudder at this idea, although you may be able to devise some form of guarantee that isn't as "radical". For example, one method I've used is to ask for a retainer up front that compensates for about 50% of the total cost. Then I tell the client they will be billed at the end of the project. If they are not satisfied with the work, they can pay whatever they feel is reasonable for the final bill. Yes, once in a while someone may take advantage of this offer.
>
> Also, on assignments that lasted a number of months, and had monthly bills, I've indicated at the outset that the customer had the opportunity to eliminate payment of the final invoice, which would result in a discount of about 20% on the entire amount.

Offering guarantees like this can help. Few will take advantage of you.

Another idea is to offer a free task up front. Break the project into a few small tasks, and do the first one at no cost. Just breaking the job into smaller phases and agreeing to have the customer authorize by phase can be a good strategy.

> *"One of the biggest 'competitive-edge' advantages you'll ever gain is to always make it easier for the client to say yes than it is for them to say no."*
> —Jay Abraham

Another risk reducer is "emotional risk reduction". Provide the customer with several testimonials from past customers who liked your work. Or, present a good case history of a successful assignment that was similar to the assignment your customer needs.

Bottom line: always include some form of risk reduction, especially to first-time buyers.

Putting It All Together

OK, we've thrown a lot of concepts and techniques at you. Now you are probably wondering how all this fits together.

When you embark upon a marketing process that supports your offering, it is critical that you systematize this process as much as possible. In other words, look at the marketing and sales effort as a system. We suggest this for two primary reasons. First, you need to take the time to map out each of the steps you will take, from initial market research to winning an assignment. Second, having a system will enable you to obtain valuable data, test the system, and make refinements as you proceed. In other words, you must be able to determine if your marketing is working optimally.

Before you begin marketing, lay out a plan, or series of steps. Here is the basic format:

1. **Offering Description**: Create a detailed description of your offering, as we discussed in Chapter 2. This

description will be the basis for your compelling marketing message.

2. **Target Market Sector**: Next, you need to establish your target market. Markets have four dimensions: demographics, geographics, psychographics, and marketgraphics.

   Demographics represents zip codes, for example, where people may live who have the characteristics you want (age, income, homeowners, culture, etc.). Or, more simply, demographics might be rural areas versus suburbs versus cities.

   Geographics identifies the location of your market. Is your market a local one where you will contact prospects within a number of miles from your location, or is it limited to a region of the country (the South, the coasts, etc.)? Are you targeting certain countries (e.g., English-speaking)?

   Psychographics deals with the psychology of your potential clients. It includes such issues as buying motives, prospects' values, their personality, educational level, job descriptions, and so on. Also, we are looking for people who are in your "tribe", as we discussed earlier. You may find these prospects in certain organizations, such as the Chamber, the Grange, the Rotary, or professional trade associations (e.g., Edison Electric Institute for electric power utility prospects).

   Marketgraphics means looking for more clients within the same, or related, market sector. For example, suppose you have clients amongst electric utility firms. You may want to target a related market sector, such as independent power producers, where your market knowledge will help you.

In summary, you want to identify a target market that is relatively narrow, or right-sized. If your market is too broad, your marketing message will not resonate well. You want to focus on one market sector to start and create a clear message for that market sector. You also want to be sure you're prepared for the jobs you accept. If you're just starting out, it's imperative that your customers are very satisfied with your performance; they are your potential testimonials that you'll use in future marketing!

3. **Customer Archetype**: A customer archetype is a group of customers that have similar characteristics. Conservatives is an example. Another example would be people who frequent fast food restaurants. One more is your current and past customers.

   You need to describe the characteristics of the prospects within your target market. What are their interests? What is their age group? Are they homeowners or renters? What types of careers do they have? What is their educational level? The more you can type this group, the better you can craft an effective marketing message to them.

4. **Compelling Marketing Message**: OK, now you are ready to compose your marketing message to your target audience. That message must address both the covert (personal or emotional) and overt (factual or logical) benefits.

   Start by researching your competition. What marketing messages do they use? What keywords

---

"Without the right sales skills, something terrible happens: nothing."
—Harvey McKay

---

do they use to describe the benefits? Look in magazines, trade journals, newspapers, blogs, websites, or wherever your target market spends time or advertises. This exercise should provide a lot of ideas.

Your marketing message should satisfy an unfulfilled need of your target market. Examples could be faster service, least expensive option, a better guarantee, or an emotional appeal (less calories, save money, more attractive, etc.). Then include your mission or your values. Stand for something.

5. **Channel Selection**: Next, select the marketing channels where your target audience hangs out. Start with one or two, and then branch out as you determine how to optimize each channel's results. The broad categories are offline and online. We discussed examples earlier.

6. **Lead Generation**: Now you need to penetrate the channels and start identifying leads, or prospects. There are two types of lead generation: direct and indirect.

   Direct lead generation is where you make contact with prospects. This includes networking, working conferences, email, direct mail, and referrals.

   Indirect lead generation includes speaking at conferences, submitting papers for publication in trade journals, advertising (offline and online), and public relations. Once again, where do your target audiences congregate?

   Try to get a response from the new prospects, either from a quick face-to-face introduction at a meeting, through a direct mail campaign, an email campaign, or an advertising campaign (Facebook, LinkedIn, or e-zines online, or trade magazines or relevant magazines offline). Remember, you will need to contact prospects several times.

7. **Lead Qualification**: Once you make an initial contact with a prospect, you will want to qualify them or disqualify them based upon some intelligence you gather about them. A qualified prospect will merit more of your time.

   Qualify prospects into at least three categories: a qualified prospect (possible buyer within 3-6 months), a possible (6-12 months), and disqualified (no authority to make a decision, no budget, or no interest in your service).

8. **Lead Conversion**: The last step in this process is to convert qualified prospects into customers. Continue to build relationships. Do this by spending time with them. Tell them your story and get the prospect to see you as them. Show the prospect the path forward: there is a problem, and here are several potential solutions. Help the prospect select the best option. Learn to write persuasive proposals.

OK, let's take a break! You are ready to complete Section 7 of your Success Roadmap. Proceed to Chapter 7 and perform this task now.

Writing Persuasively

The last topic we will cover in this chapter is writing with intent to win. First, we will discuss persuasive writing, and then we will describe the basics of proposal preparation. Proposals are the primary mechanism consultants use to sell.

Here are some suggestions to keep in mind when writing sales material.

▶ **Situational Analysis**: Understand your prospect's situation. What is their key concern... what frustrates them... what worries them... what is getting in the way of success? Next, what do they really want? Do they want to save (time, money, effort)... gain (more profitability, higher revenues)... feel better about... earn more respect (recognition)... more control... more freedom?

▶ **Key Benefits**: People don't buy things; they buy results. What is the biggest result provided by your offer? What needs are not being fulfilled? What frustrations can be eliminated? Look at the emotional side first.

▶ **Educate:** Education is the benevolent way to sell. Educate the prospect about their own problem. Explain it better than they can. Educate the prospect about the potential solutions to their problem. Educate the prospect about the benefits of each potential solution.

▶ **Dispel Myths/Destroy Objections**: To identify objections, first look very closely at your service. Frankly analyze your offer and list the major negatives. No offer is perfect. What issues regarding your offer will instill some doubt about buying? Too complicated? Too much time to complete? Too good to be true? Second, look at your service from the perspective of

> *"Share from your heart.*
> *And your story will touch*
> *and heal people's souls."*
>
> *Melody Beattie*

the prospect. Why would they pause before buying? Price too high? Guarantee not strong enough? Not enough free stuff to attract interest?

► **Motivate**: There are two general approaches to motivating a buyer: pain and gain. Most marketers think that leading with pain is better. In that case, pose the key problem faced by the prospect. Show why this problem hurts the prospect. Find some corroborating third party data that reinforces the problem. Then present a solution that removes the pain.

A second approach begins with the gain. How will the prospect benefit from your service or product? How will your service help the company your prospects work for? Show how the prospect will benefit personally. Show how others are already benefitting. After motivating with one of these approaches, add scarcity, reciprocity, social proof, authority, or other persuasion techniques we've discussed.

► **Appearance**: Make your document interesting to read. Do this by using lots of white space, graphics, photographs with captions, bold fonts, highlighting, indenting, short paragraphs, and bullet lists. Write like you talk (informal). Use the active voice (lots of verbs). Pose questions and answer them.

► **Tell a Story:** Everyone loves a story, whether it is in books, movies, speeches, or even marketing materials like brochures and proposals. When you tell a story about yourself, or someone else who had a problem similar to that being faced by your prospect, the prospect begins to put himself/herself in the story. Tell how the character in the story confronted challenges, overcame them, and found a solution. They start to identify with the person in the story (you!). Stories that inspire are one of the most effective sales techniques!

We want to apply these persuasive writing techniques to our proposals. Writing proposals may be the most important writing that a consultant does. Let's address the proposal preparation process for a moment before concluding this chapter.

Here is a framework for preparing proposals:

1. Planning
2. Strategy Development
3. Design
4. Production
5. Delivery & Follow-up

Each of these steps is briefly described below.

1. **Planning**: As soon as you see a proposal opportunity coming, begin gathering intelligence. How do you gather intelligence? Meet with your client. That's the best way. Also, ask other contractors who have worked for this client before. Talk to retired employees who used to work at the firm. It is important to determine your potential weaknesses early and bring consultants on board before they are swallowed up by other bidders. That's why we emphasize forming the team in the first step.

   Also, once the opportunity arrives, conduct a go no-go analysis to determine if you should pursue the opportunity. Do you have the appropriate staff available? Do you have an attractive project manager available? Can you make money on this project? Do any of your competitors work for this client? Do they have an inside track for this opportunity? If you're just starting out, it may be hard to turn down any opportunity. But the go no-go analysis is about spending your marketing time well. You're deciding if what you're seeing is a real opportunity, or something on which you could spend a lot of time without any real chance of success. Learning when to say "no-go" will earn you time, money, and more satisfied clients in the long run.

2. **Strategy Development**: Two key issues are what benefits you can offer the prospect, and how you can differentiate from your competition. Most importantly, you must determine the prospect's "hot button" issues, or the ones that really matter to them. The best way to find hot buttons is to ask! Other ways include looking at the proposal evaluation criteria, the prospect's history dealing with this issue or problem, published plans that show their goals, or political issues that may have impacted the prospect. With regard to your competition, it's always helpful to discuss optional approaches to the scope of work, for example, and eliminate the approach your competitors will take.

In addition, include the advantages you bring to the table, such as a well-qualified project manager, special team qualifications, unique or innovative work scope, or expedited schedule.

When you have all of your hot buttons, create a compelling proposal theme, such as "Proven

Approach to Sidewalk Widening Design Wins Unanimous Council Support".

3. **Design**: In this step, start with a work breakdown structure (this is a logical listing of the tasks that form the basis for the work flow required). Then, design the document, including artwork, resumes, project abstracts, project organization chart, cover art, and graphics. Create a very specific production schedule so that the document is available for review, careful proofreading or editing, and then final copying. The biggest mistake many make is to rush through the final steps and produce a document that has typos, or worse, an unclear offer that doesn't respond to the client's needs.

The proposal should address the following subjects, either as separate sections for a major proposal, or within the text for shorter proposals:

o Introduction (make your sales pitch, build credibility)
o Problem Statement (concise definition with success criteria)
o Scope of Work (work breakdown structure, assumptions)
o Methodology (describe each task/subtask, with deliverables)
o Project Organization (team qualifications, project controls)
o Qualifications (by client, expertise, scope, location)
o Schedule (key milestones, critical path issues)
o Cost (risk reversal, how costs are controlled, justify high cost)

4. **Production**: Make a draft copy for review. Make the changes, and perform a final edit. Good writing skills are important (and something you should continually work to improve), but even the best writer finds it extremely difficult to proof their own writing. It's just how the brain works. Have a friend or staff member read your proposal, or find a good editor—a professional or a friend or business associate willing to team up with you—and get their feedback. Ask them if anything seemed unclear, and to offer corrections for any errors they notice. Produce your first "final" hardcopy and conduct a page turn, and correct any errors you see. Then print the final hardcopies, CDs, or pdf files—whatever format your client requested.

5. **Delivery & Follow-up**: Deliver the proposal in person one day early if possible. Then you may be able to get some initial feedback, and make any changes recommended by the client. Follow up soon after the proposal is delivered to let the client know you stand ready to answer any questions or provide additional information. It never hurts to let them know you're available and ready to communicate.

6. Always **have a back-up** method of getting the proposal in on time. During my career, at least two times Fed Ex did not deliver overnight on time.

Marketing on the Internet

The Internet is a relatively new place for marketing your services. However, it is rapidly becoming a must-do task for most consultants. In fact, there are thousands of consultants who depend upon the Internet for 100% of their business. Here are a few reasons why the Internet has become an important venue for marketing:

1. The Internet provides you with almost instant access to potential customers worldwide. And, you can target your customers with laser accuracy.

2. The Internet medium also is changing quickly, so it's worth the effort to stay abreast of the latest technology, marketing techniques, and networking tools or services like Facebook, LinkedIn, Spoke, and many others.

3. Internet marketing is great for small firms and sole proprietorships (individuals). For relatively low cost you can reach your targeted audience.

4. There are many marketing channels on the Internet. You must determine which ones work best for your service and target audience by testing them and evaluating your return on investment (e.g., pay per click and pay per conversion).

5. It is still quite easy and inexpensive to establish a website on the Internet. And, if you don't want to spend the time setting up your website, or even designing it, you can engage consultants to help at astonishingly low costs. Try vworker. com or elance.com. Be careful not to outsource your sales messaging. You know best what your service is, and how it can benefit prospects. And as you probably know by your own research, "everyone" has a website these days. It's an

expected resource for a business, and potential clients may check you out online by looking at your website.

6. Finally—and it should go without saying—the Internet can be an *anti*-marketing tool. Your potential clients may not share your political or religious views, or they may be uncomfortable to learn you participate in "unconventional" activities that could reduce your value to them. So be attentive to how you post on your social networking sites. You want to be sure that you present yourself well even on sites you consider more casual or not related to business. (Have you heard about the employees who have been fired because they posted about illegal activities on their Facebook pages? You *never* want that kind of story to be about you!)

So those are some of the many reasons the Internet is an important tool. *But it is only a tool; the Internet is not a substitute for interacting with people directly.* If you are, or become active marketing your service on the Internet, you will want to continue to attend relevant conferences where you can find new ideas and identify more leads. The Internet can be an efficient lead generation tool and education tool, but the consultant with the edge is the one who has developed live, personal relationships with potential clients.

With that introduction, we will look at the Internet from two perspectives: to get sales, and to market your services.

Online Sales Processes

Online sales are booming, particularly when selling to individuals (as opposed to firms). However, as we learned earlier in this chapter, we should not rely on just one channel for all of our sales.

Here is a six-step framework for selling services on the Internet:

1. Target Your Audience
2. Develop Your Sales Message
3. Establish Your Web Presence
4. Drive Traffic to Your Site
5. Connect with Your List
6. Sell Services to Your List

Steps 1 and 2 are similar to those we have discussed for any market channel, and Step 3 should reflect your brand—the logo on your business cards, the fonts you use for stationery, etc. Consistency is valuable. Steps 4-6 are more specific to the Internet.

Let's discuss each of these steps.

Target Your Audience: Probably the most important step is this first one. You must carefully target your audience. Examples could be your past clients, existing clients, businesses close to your geographical location, a target market segment (e.g., electric utilities), or people who are members of an organization, such as your Chamber of Commerce, or a professional association. If you're not sure what associations are out there, just Google "professional associations". Many websites list associations sorted by business category (information technology, consulting, advertising, religion, travel, etc.). You'll find many professional associations related to your field.

Your target audience should be as close to you as possible in terms of educational background, interests and hobbies, financial standing, family orientation, and so on. Yes, essentially, you are looking for you!

Develop Your Sales Message: Now that you have identified your target audience, you must design an effective sales message that will engage them. Your sales message must address several purposes: grab their attention, gain their interest, pull them further into a conversation, sell them on your concept, and get them to take action. Remember, a sales message cannot appeal to everyone. That is why you selected a focused target audience!

Here are a few pointers to craft a good sales message:

▶ **Tell a story**. Everyone likes a story. Stories help the reader relate to you.

▶ **Educating** is a great way to persuade. Educate them about your qualifications and accomplishments, their problem and your solution.

▶ Don't just provide information or facts about your service. You must *motivate* **your prospect**. What are the key emotional motivators that drive the prospect? Is it to earn more money? Do they want a better lifestyle? Do they want more security?

▶ **Convert the value you offer in your service into a benefit for the prospect**. In my site selection business, for example, we say that using our siting expertise will result in the identification of better sites that will be permitted and constructed sooner, and earning revenue faster.

▶ **Clarity is key.** One way to increase clarity is to break your sales message into a number of small steps or phases.

▶ Of course, it is always helpful to include scarcity (only 20 are available, so buy now!).

Establish Your Web Presence: Your website is like a catalog. It contains a description of all of your services, along with the benefits of using them. You might have case histories where you show how you helped clients. You might include testimonials from satisfied clients. You may include appealing offers, discounts, or incentives.

There are two broad categories of website designs: a squeeze page and a landing page. A squeeze page has only one objective: get the visitor's name and email. This is usually done by offering a valuable gift, such as an e-book or a newsletter, in exchange for signing up. A landing page contains a detailed sales letter that describes your service and benefits. The landing page is more applicable to professionals because it takes some effort to educate people about your service.

It has become very easy to build a web presence. Most websites are created using Wordpress, the industry standard. You can host your website with a number of hosting companies like Go Daddy or Host Gator. If you need help, ask your business associates who designed their websites, or post a job ad in Elance.

Drive Traffic to Your Site: There are two general types of traffic you can generate toward your site: organic and paid. Organic traffic is created through the use of search engine optimization (SEO), commenting on blogs, submitting articles to article databases and sites like www.ezinearticles. com, uploading videos on Youtube or Tubemogul, and otherwise creating incoming and outgoing links to your website. This activity gets you recognized in Google, increases your ranking, and drives traffic.

With regard to paid traffic, ads can be purchased on Facebook, LinkedIn, Yahoo, and other sites. These ads, which comprise a brief heading, an image, and brief body text, are structured to encourage people to click on them and be sent to your website, where they have the opportunity to opt-in (i.e., provide their name and email address). Typically, you must offer some valuable free material to get good conversion (opt-ins).

You also can create traffic through email marketing, where you rent a list of people interested in your service. Your emails would include an invitation to visit your website and opt-in. You can also advertise on the Internet using banner ads.

If you are offering professional services, you must have a profile on LinkedIn, where you are company to over 100 million professionals. LinkedIn has a number of ways to interact with others on the site, such as company sites and groups.

Connect with Your List: Once you begin building a list, you must frequently communicate with them through emails. Many people publish a simple e-newsletter containing tips and news about their specialty.

Sell Services to Your List: The last step is to start selling to your list! There are a number of ways to do this. Here are four of my favorites:

▶ **Sell on your website**. As mentioned above, your website is your catalog. Include detailed descriptions of your services and their benefits. This is a common approach.

▶ **Sell through emails**. You can make offers in an email. This is another common method.

▶ **Sell through a series of emails**. In this method, you send three or four emails that provide valuable information to the prospect. For example, you might present an overview of your service in terms of a four-step plan. Describe each step in an email. In your last email, make the offer. This sequence builds trust.

▶ **Sell through emails that lead to a webinar**. This method is similar to the previous one, except that you end with a live or recorded webinar. Webinars are good sales vehicles if your service is more complex, or requires more explanation. Also, a webinar affords you the time to get into details that would not be practical in an email. Live webinars, of course, have more excitement.

Now that you have finished this chapter it's time to complete sections 8 (Sales Plan) and 9 (Proposal Template) in your Success Roadmap!

4. Problem Solving for Consultants

When most consultants perform a service, they are typically solving a problem for the customer. As a result, problem solving becomes a critical skill for consultants. Yet, you don't find many courses in problem solving.

During my long consulting career I found problem solving to be one of the most important skills, and a skill that was critical to the success of most projects. In this chapter, we will introduce the topic, talk about a problem solving mindset, provide an overview of problem solving processes, present two building blocks for solving problems, and finish with the problem solving framework.

Keep in mind that "problem solving" includes "finding opportunities". As a consultant, clients ask that you solve problems. However, there is even more value in finding opportunities; opportunities to anticipate problem formation, improve processes or create new and better processes.

"Values are what we care about. As such, values should be the driving force for our decision-making."
—Ralph Keeney

Generally speaking, we can look at the problem solving process as having three components:

▶ problem initiation,

▶ problem analysis, and

▶ solution development.

One can define a number of steps within each of these components, as we shall see. However, before getting into the weeds, there are three aspects of problem solving that often do not get the attention they deserve:

▶ objectives development,

▶ alternatives analysis, and

▶ decision-making.

First, let's consider objectives. What are problem objectives? They convey what is important about a problem. More specifically, an objective is a statement about what the decision-maker wants to achieve. Importantly, objectives reflect our values.

For example, if we wanted to improve the operations of the local police department, we could take one of two paths. First, we could look at what's not working and seek to improve the department—in other words, go right at the problem. This is how we typically solve problems. Or, we could look at the basic objectives of the department (e.g., protect residents, enforce the laws, investigate crime, provide emergency assistance). This is what the residents *value* in a police department. Then we could consider the ways in which we could achieve these objectives. By starting with the objectives, we likely would end up defining many more alternatives to improving the police force. We would focus on the right issues, the issues that matter most to us.

My point here is that few consultants start a problem-solving process by considering the objectives behind the problem. When you begin the problem solving process by considering the objectives, it will change the way you approach problem solving.

The second aspect of problem solving that is often neglected is alternatives formation. In most cases, the obvious solution is acted upon. Little effort is expended to define a complete set of alternatives based upon the objectives, as we listed for the police department. You will find that expending that effort will yield much better, and more effective, problem solutions.

The third aspect of problem solving is decision-making. At some point in the problem solving process, you must make a decision. Oddly enough, most consultants—indeed, most people—never have been taught how to make a decision. However, I think you will agree that decision-making is one of the most important activities a consultant will perform. For example, deciding which alternative problem solution is best for a client is a critical aspect of problem solving.

We will address these issues again later in this chapter when we discuss the problem solving framework.

The Problem-solving Mindset

When you begin to consider a problem situation, it helps to put your mind into a problem-solving state. Put another way, here are a few pointers when you get started on a problem assignment:

▶ **Challenge anchored thinking**. In other words, challenge the conventional wisdom, and biases. Think outside the box. It is easy to anchor, or short-circuit your thinking because an apparent solution presents itself early, especially if proposed by the client. Now, I am not saying the client is wrong; I am just saying be careful. Anchored thinking is, simply put, the way someone already tends to solve a problem. If that habitual way of approaching a problem provided your client the perfect solution, he wouldn't have elected to hire you. The client can be biased, just as you can. Also, note that your past experience can anchor your own thoughts about new solutions. Just being aware of how the mind anchors thinking will help you counteract it.

▶ **Be sure to seek out divergent views**. This pointer is complementary to the first one. The root of creativity and a source of creative solutions is exposure to different views. If someone is strongly proposing a solution, be sure to get other opinions, or review the facts carefully to see if other alternatives may exist.

I've had clients who engaged me to essentially confirm a decision they'd already made. They were looking for an outside consultant to back up their solution to a problem. In these cases, it is important to tread softly, yet work to create a list of alternative solutions.

▶ **Suspend judgment until all data is collected**. If someone is pushing you into a decision or position, say, "Let me have some time to consider your point". Be careful about making quick judgments... they are usually the result of a "gut feel", which may not rely on all of the facts. Remember the saying, "Fools rush in where angels fear to tread."

▶ **Differentiate facts from opinions.** Be careful to separate facts from opinions when making decisions. Ask an opinionated person to back up their opinion with some facts. Always find out where the data, or facts, originated. What is the source? Some people may think that asking this question is confrontational or argumentative; nothing could be further from the truth. You simply want to be as informed as you can, and you want the opportunity to review data to better educate yourself.

▶ **Separate the relevant data from the irrelevant.** Focus on the important issues and data that are directly related to the problem. Don't get sidetracked by issues, or data, that do not affect the analysis of the problem. If you're in doubt, ask how an offered piece of information might affect the problem.

"It's not the right answers that are important in problem solving, it is asking the right questions."

—Peter Drucker

▶ **Ask "what if" questions to challenge or change thinking patterns.** Asking questions is a powerful tool for uncovering data. We discuss this tool in the next section.

▶ **Take time for reflection/independent thought.** I was recently in a client meeting where there was a consensus on a solution to a method of generating power at a landfill. The client staff seemed well prepared and offered this solution. Everything sounded good. Maybe too good. I asked for a recess in the meeting. During the recess, I took a closer look at the staff's analysis. I challenged the assumption of the quantity of biomass that would be available. I didn't have time in the meeting to review the data. The recess was helpful.

Always take the time to evaluate the situation yourself. This is what you are being paid for.

The Power of Questions

As Peter Drucker said, we must ask the *right* questions. When attacking a problem, start by asking a lot of questions. Typically, it will help to focus on the following subjects.

- ▶ **Objectives**: Remember our example of the police department, and how objectives are closely related to values? Objectives are bottom-line reasons why we are concerned about a given situation. What are the overall objectives? What are the major concerns? The best decisions are made by identifying, and considering the achievement of, objectives.

- ▶ **Methods and Procedures**: Are the correct procedures being applied? Have standards been published for procedures being applied?

- ▶ **Technology**: Is the appropriate technology being utilized? Technology changes very rapidly. Is the latest technology being used? If the work is overseen by a regulatory agency, do they specify a technology or type of equipment that must be used?

► **Communication**: Is communication on the project a barrier? Are the individuals involved in the project communicating effectively? Is the communication sufficiently frequent to avoid misunderstanding? From my experience, this is the chief cause of mistakes in projects.

► **Time**: Is the lack of time an issue? First, many poor decisions have resulted because the decision-makers were under time pressures. Don't be afraid of asking for more time if needed to reach a quality decision. Second, if we don't keep an eye on progress, we may slip on the project schedule. Anticipate time issues early.

► **Cost**: Is cost an issue? Is there sufficient budget to carry out the required tasks? If cost is limited, has the scope been controlled to be consistent with the budget? Has the budget been allocated to the most critical tasks? Cost mismanagement is a common problem that can be avoided by monitoring expenditures and projecting expenditures for the remainder of the project.

► **People**: Are there persons who need to be consulted? Is the project team properly constructed? Are all of the experts required present on the team?

► **Materials & Resources**: Are the required materials for solving the problem being made available? Are resources ready when you need them?

These types of questions also often help define a problem.

Problem-solving Processes

Problem solving has been around for thousands of years. Processes used to solve problems have evolved over time.

Most problems encountered today can be solved in three basic ways:

▶ Trial and error,

▶ The use of heuristics, and

▶ The use of algorithms.

All problem solving began, a long time ago, with trial and error. Children specialize in trial and error. It is natural for them. We use trial and error when we can't identify a better way. It is our fallback approach if nothing else works. Trial and error is akin to walking through a maze. Many mistakes are made, and lots of time is typically required (look at Edison and the light bulb). Trial and error is not helpful in high-risk situations (e.g., defusing a bomb). So, generally, trial and error isn't too helpful for us consultants. Our customers expect more!

Heuristics are rules that people have devised over the years that point to a more efficient solution, based upon past experience and in some cases, based on trial and error. We will address a few of these rules, including working backwards (reverse engineering), frameworks, cause and effect, and brainstorming.

The third problem-solving method utilizes algorithms. An algorithm takes a heuristic a bit further and specifies a step-by-step procedure to attain the desired result. Simple examples are division and multiplication. Other examples include linear programming and decision analysis. I have found decision analysis to be *extremely* useful in consulting because it centers on finding the *best* result, not just a result that works. Also, decision analysis teaches you to be very logical and systematic. Clients love logic and systematic approaches. Why? They are easy to understand!

Before discussing the problem solving framework, we'll define a couple tools that will help problem solving.

Problem-solving Building Blocks

I've found that three tools are especially helpful in problem solving. When you are confronted with a problem, especially a complex problem, it is beneficial to express the problem situation in a form that promotes understanding. I've found frameworks, systems and processes, and decision trees to be useful in problem solving.

▶ **Frameworks** are great for demonstrating understanding of a problem. They are 50,000-foot-level problem depictions. Frameworks show what tasks or processes are involved, and how they interrelate.

▶ **Systems and Processes** help you understand the relationship between problem components or issues. The use of systems and processes is just a subset of a framework, or one type of framework.

▶ **Decision Trees** are an excellent tool to aid in thinking through a problem. Let's drill down a bit further into frameworks, systems, and decision analysis.

I've seen many definitions of the word "framework." Among them are:

▶ A framework is a roadmap, a template, a model, or, a general depiction of an activity.

▶ Frameworks can describe how and why we perform an activity.

▶ Frameworks indicate what things mean and how they work.

▶ Frameworks show a client that you fully understand a situation, and that you have probably at least seen, if not solved, this problem before.

Frameworks help *you* understand the situation! The first thing you want to do when confronted with a problem is to construct a framework and see if it makes sense to you. If it doesn't, that likely is a signal that some information is missing.

Frameworks break down complex concepts into easy to understand "maps" or models. Whoops! I think I just slipped in yet another definition of a framework!

An excellent example of a framework is Steven Covey's *Seven Habits of Effective People* framework. When Covey was conceptualizing the idea of habits of successful people, he first created this framework. His entire book on this subject follows this framework... a roadmap, if you will.

You can see that a framework can be a useful device. It puts an idea, especially a complex idea, into a perspective that enhances understanding.

Systems and processes are another way to conceptualize a situation. Let's look at a couple of definitions to start.

A system is a collection of processes that combine in some organized fashion to produce a higher order output.

A process is a defined work activity that has an input, a value-added work activity, and an output.

The insert shows a system with an input, four work activities, or processes, and an output.

A useful tool for describing or conceptualizing a problem situation can be a process model. In a process model, everyone is a client (receives an output from another process). In addition, everyone owns a process or processes. In other words, whatever you do can be defined as a process. And finally, everyone is a supplier to another

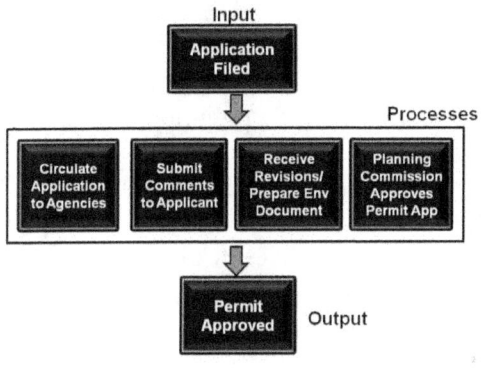

process in a system. Whatever you do in your job is done for someone. You become a supplier to their process.

For example, suppose you process vendor invoices in an accounting department. Your process is reviewing invoices, making sure they comply with standards, and ensuring that there are sufficient funds in project budgets to pay them. Your suppliers are project managers, who need to get their vendor invoices paid. Your clients are the clients of the firm, who expect you to pay the invoices. The vendors you're paying are the project managers' suppliers... and so on. Also, note that your process is controlled by procedures, and there is likely a process above yours in the system.

To improve a process, it must be well understood. Again, this is a great first step in problem solving. Once you have a depiction of the process or processes involved in a problem situation, you are in a much better position to understand the problem.

Lastly, we will briefly mention *decision trees* as a thinking concept. Decision trees are "decision support tools" that can be used to show alternative strategies or options. More complex versions show alternative strategies along with probabilities and outcomes for each "branch".

An example of a decision tree is shown in the insert. Carbon dioxide can be sequestered (stored) underground. The insert shows the key impacts that can result from sequestration, including oil & gas deposits, surface water contamination, water aquifer contamination, and air pollution.

For each key impact, the tree shows more details about the impacts. For example, with regard to atmospheric (air pollution) impacts, a consequence is livestock damage (deaths from carbon dioxide suffocation). The next boxes show the ultimate consequence—in this case, possible claims on livestock damage.

We can add more complexity to this tree by showing probabilities that certain impacts could occur, and adding the costs of the consequences. When we add this detail, we can make more informed decisions.

With these "building blocks" in mind, now it is time to introduce the consultant's problem-solving framework, which is the basis for solving a client's problem. We will discuss a nine-step process everyone can use to help solve any problem.

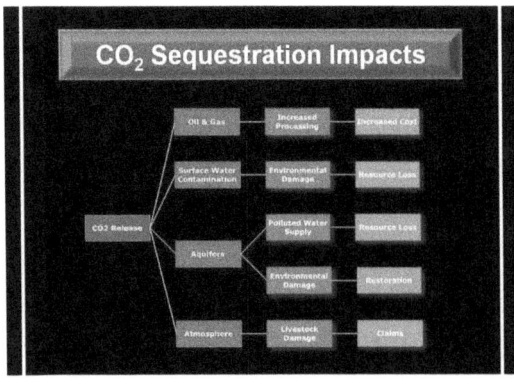

I've used a problem solving process countless times over the years, as you have.

When I began solving problems for my clients, this process had only a few steps. However, as I gained more experience, I added more steps. Why? I discovered that we automatically addressed some steps, rather than considering each with the same level of attention and detail.

If you follow each of the nine steps described below, it will significantly improve your problem solving ability. It will take some practice, however. Practice them with your family on problems in the home, or with your staff and business partners on real or made-up problems with your business practice. Everyone wins from improved problem solving skills!

To make this process easier to describe and understand, it is separated into three groups of three steps that I introduced at the beginning of this chapter: Project Initiation (steps 1-3), Problem Analysis (steps 4-6), and Solution Development (steps 7-9).

Consultant's Problem-solving Framework

This framework consists of the following nine steps:

1. Problem Finding

2. Problem Identification

3. Problem Definition

4. Problem Assessment

5. Data Collection

6. Data Analysis

7. Alternative Solution Identification

8. Solution Evaluation

9. Solution Selection

Steps 1-3 are used to initiate the problem-solving process. This includes finding the problem, identifying the problem, and defining the problem. Most of us do these steps automatically in our heads. However, if you recognize these individual steps, and think about them, you should improve your problem-solving ability.

Steps 4-6 we call "problem analysis". This is where we delve into the problem, understand it better, and characterize it properly. In many cases, this requires collection of more data and compilation of the data into a spreadsheet, and expressed graphically, for example.

Steps 7-9 we call "solution development". In these steps, we start by identifying a set of potential solutions. Then we evaluate these options, and finally, we go through a decision-making process to enable us to select the best solution for the customer.

Problem Initiation

Dr. Ralph Keeney, in his book entitled *Value-Focused Thinking*, covers the steps in problem initiation very well. Project initiation includes problem finding, problem identification, and project definition.

Problem finding (Step 1) deals with the question of which problem should be solved. In other words, make sure you are solving the CORRECT problem. Problem finding also deals with scanning goals, values, and needs to see if they are being satisfied. Note that goals are desired outcomes identified in a planning activity, so goals are often a source of problems (namely, not attaining them!). Finally, problem finding involves looking for opportunities, or what we might call incipient problems.

Values are what we place importance on. Values, therefore, are a critical consideration in problem solving and especially, in decision-making. Values represent personal or business-oriented preferences for desired outcomes. A business value might be "our employees share their knowledge with other staff". Explicit consideration of values will stimulate, and vastly improve, the problem-finding process.

In summary, problem finding can be reactive or proactive. In the reactive mode, you are ensuring that the right problem is being solved. Also, you may recognize a problem because of a trigger, such as an upcoming date when a regulatory response is due, or notification of an alert from a system monitor.

Proactive problem finding involves searching for process improvements, or creating a plan that includes the need for an action. This type of problem finding is also called opportunity finding, an activity that is very important in consulting.

Next, a problem is *identified* (Step 2) when the gap between the current situation and the expected state reaches an action, or trigger, level. We can define a problem as a gap between the current situation and the desired situation. When such a gap is identified, a problem is identified, or found. When evaluating a problem situation, or trying to determine if there is a problem, use the gap test: Is there a gap between the current situation and the desired situation?

Problems can be identified when comparing predicted or desired outcomes contained in a planning document. Or, a problem is identified when a metric is compared to historical data. For example, if the Gross Domestic Product (GDP) declines three quarters in a row, we call it a recession.

And finally, a Problem Statement, or *Problem Definition* (Step 3), must be created to codify the problem. The problem definition should have a context, an object, and a direction. The context is a simple statement of the current state (e.g., unemployment is too high, which creates dislocation and instability). The object is a data point of reference (e.g., the existing unemployment rate is 8.1%). The direction is the trend you are looking for, increasing, decreasing, minimizing, maximizing, etc. (e.g., we want the unemployment rate to decrease). Make sure that when you define a problem, you include all three parts.

Problem Analysis

The Problem Analysis steps include problem assessment, data collection, and data analysis (and compilation).

In *Problem Assessment* (Step 4), we look at the symptoms, causes, and root causes that are related to the problem. Essentially, we want to understand the relationship between the causes and the problem, being careful to distinguish between causes and symptoms.

Looking at the insert, we are examining why a person cannot find a job. The "5 Whys" is a useful tool for uncovering causes. One cause is the lack of job openings. However, a root cause, or deeper level cause, is that the job seeker doesn't have the right expertise, which reduces the job opportunities. Digging deeper, he didn't take the proper courses (root cause). Another example of a root cause for the same situation might be, "the market changed dramatically due to regulations or a changed political environment." There is no "one right answer"; the answer depends almost entirely on the specific problem being addressed.

A symptom, on the other hand, could be a lack of leads entering your sales funnel. A cause could be that potential prospects are not being attracted by your sales message. A root cause could be a poorly targeted market sector or poor sales message.

Most causes occur as physical, human, or organizational. Many human causes (e.g., a driver does not stop at a traffic light) turn into physical causes (a traffic accident). There are many potential organizational causes of problems, such as system instability, poor policies, poor procedures, poor implementation of existing good policies or procedures, and ineffective communication or management.

Another useful tool in root cause analysis is the Cause and Effect Diagram, more affectionately called the Fishbone Diagram. I've used this tool many times in client meetings. It is especially helpful when considering one decision or action.

This tool is a graphic representation of the relationship between an effect (the problem) and its potential causes. It also can be used to identify and sort the success factors or improvement opportunities in a process.

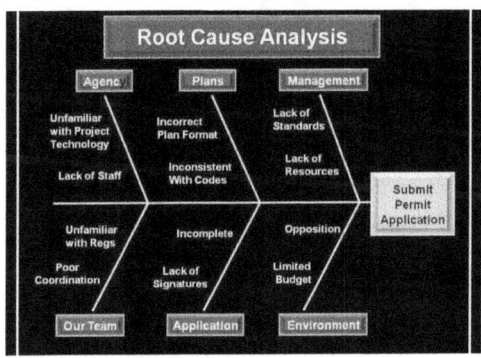

See the Fishbone Diagram in the insert. This example shows the cause of permitting delays on a new project. Notice that the diagram addresses several overall issues: the regulatory agency, the project plans, management's role in the project, the project team's work, the permit application itself, and the environmental impacts. These are the "top-level" issues. In most applications of the Fishbone Diagram, you will want to include such issues as people, the environment, materials, equipment, and work procedures, as applied to your project, as we did in the example.

In *Data Collection* (Step 5), we collect additional data that may be needed to properly evaluate a situation. Make a clear path between data and the problem. In other words, make sure that the data are correlated with the problem.

> *"I keep six serving men They taught me all I know Their names are What and Why and When And How and Where and Who"*
>
> —*Rudyard Kipling on Problem Solving*

Is the data time sensitive? This could mean two things: Is the data still good, given its age, or is the data only applicable to certain times? Biological monitoring data for the siting of a construction project, for example, is typically time sensitive, because it must be collected in the spring. Other reasons for time sensitivity may be deadlines, windows of opportunity to access a property or people, etc. Determining whether data is still good is subject to the specific problems at hand. (Health and life insurance companies still use actuarial tables created decades ago. Many folks think that information is too old and should be revisited, but it still influences insurance markets today.)

Be willing to challenge the data integrity. In other words, make sure that the data is correct. Always know the source

Control Chart: Invoice Processing Days

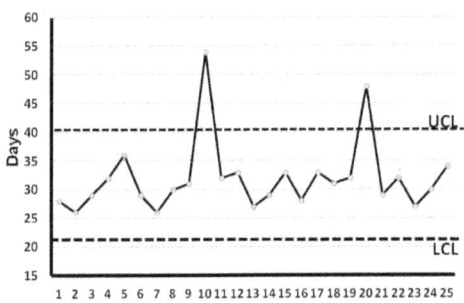

of the data. This is always a must to be sure your data are credible. Always proof the data.

Is the data a problem contributor or symptom? Make sure that the data is related to the problem, and not to a symptom of the problem. Data describing the amount of water collected inside a basement describes a symptom. The problem is that the basement walls or water flow outside the building were poorly designed. So the data you need is structural information about the basement walls, and how rainwater flows or collects outside of the basement.

Finally, organize the data with a timeline. This can be very helpful, especially for complex problems. For example, data timing is critical when assessing soil or groundwater contamination, which changes over time.

Examples of data collection methods include surveys, interviews, polls, observations, and questionnaires.

In *Data Analysis* (Step 6), we evaluate the data to see what it tells us… how the data enhance or explain the problem situation. Examples of data analysis tools are simple statistics (e.g., averages, means), multi-variate statistics (analysis of variance, regression), and graphical analysis (scatterplots, histograms, etc.). Oftentimes, just listing the data in a spreadsheet, and performing simple operations such as ordering, ranking, or averages, can yield important relationships.

We'll show one data analysis tool here, called a "control chart." This is a simple data analysis method, and valuable insights can result from its use. A few years ago, a consulting office was upsetting our relationships with vendors (suppliers) because vendor invoices were being paid late. As a first step, we diagrammed how vendor invoice processing occurred. Each process was included (logging in invoices, interacting with project managers, checking budgets, approving, etc.). Then we monitored the process for several weeks, and plotted the time each invoice spent in the process. That plot is shown here.

You can see that most of the invoices were paid within the standard of 30 days. However, there were occasional spikes up to 40-55 days. We discovered that the spikes occurred when a temporary employee stood in for an absent full-time employee.

These simple plots can be quite helpful in gaining insights into process performance.

Solution Development

The final three steps in the Problem-solving Framework are Alternative Solution Identification, Solution Evaluation, and Solution Selection.

We begin this third and last group of steps with *Alternative Solution Identification* (Step 7), where we focus on building a complete list of alternative solutions. This step is often neglected by consultants because either the client or the consultant believes that the solution is obvious, or it is assumed to be the best solution.

Keeney (*Value Focused Thinking*) describes two approaches to alternative solution identification: Alternative-based thinking and values-based thinking. Alternative-based thinking is reactive, in that you are confronted with a problem, and you must generate some solution options. Value-based thinking, on the other hand, is proactive, in that considering values early in the problem assessment process may reveal other problems, or may help to better define the problem. Remember our police department example? Starting with the values of the project (or client or firm), you may find other problems leading to identifying improvements that in turn will provide a better result than anticipated.

An example of values-based thinking is the consideration of a municipal waste incineration system. One value may be to reduce byproducts as much as possible because they can be costly to dispose. However, this may prompt a look at productive use of the by-products, which could increase revenues and make the entire project look better.

I suggest a two-part process to identify solution alternatives:

▶ Part 1: Specify the Problem Objectives (applying values), and

▶ Part 2: Create alternatives that will meet those objectives.

If you follow this approach, you'll be more likely to identify better alternatives.

The second step in solution development (Step 8 of the problem solving process) is *Solution Evaluation*. Here we carefully characterize each proposed solution so that we understand the solution and its consequences should it be implemented. It can be helpful to begin the characterization process by looking at the following factors that could influence the decision regarding the best solution:

1. **Past Experience**: Most importantly, your past experience will shade your decision making, because your brain accesses this information to help you decide. Our brain is wired to not repeat the mistakes of the past. Remember that when working with customers, their decisions are colored by experience as well.

2. **Values**: Clearly, your values will influence how you decide. In fact, I believe that these values need to be out front when decisions are made.

3. **Available Data**: Decisions will be dependent upon the data at hand. Therefore, always be sure that the data set is as complete as possible.

4. **Skills of the Team**: The skills of the decision-makers will govern, to some extent, how decisions will be made. This is especially important with respect to skills in decision-making. This is why we spend time on this subject. You, as a consultant, must lead your customer in the decision-making process.

5. **Systematic versus Intuitive**: There are two parts of our brain that help us to make decisions: the intuitive side, and the rational side, as described by Jonah Lehrer, author of *How We Decide*. These are key aspects of how we make decisions. Our rational brain focuses on the facts of the problem, while our intuitive brain focuses on patterns and emotional concerns about the problem. People use these faculties in different ways. The key point is that EVERY decision is based, in part, on your emotions, or feelings.

6. **Detail versus Pattern Oriented**: As you know, some people like to get lost in the weeds of detail, where others prefer to stay aloft and just look at patterns or rely on their intuition. Be cognizant of how people on your team, and the client, tend to evaluate situations.

> *"Nothing is more difficult, and, therefore, precious, than to be able to decide."*
>
> —*Napoleon Bonaparte*

In summary, keep these issues in mind when working with your customers.

Next, you should characterize each alternative solution using several metrics, such as environmental impacts (air, water, subsurface), economics (construction and operation), and impacts upon people (living standards, health). The purpose here is to show what the intended and unintended consequences will be for each alternative solution.

The last step (Step 9) is *solution selection*. We have several optional solutions (i.e., alternatives), and we have characterized them in terms of a few metrics. Now it is time to decide which option is best for the client. We need to make a decision!

We typically make decisions following one of these generalized rules:

1. **Gut feel**: Everyone is aware of making decisions using gut feel. It means making decisions quickly on past information. It can be a rush to judgment. However, gut feel does involve values. Gut feel relies on intuition (intuition is a mix of values and experience). Many great decisions have been made this way. However, as a consultant,

you need decision methods that can withstand tough scrutiny.

2. **Facts**: Aside from gut feel, most decisions are made based on facts. There are many decision-support tools that help us make the best decisions. Be careful, however, not to avoid values if the decision requires them! And recall that *all* decisions by humans involve feelings.

3. **Values-based**: Also, we can make values-based decisions. In many decision situations, company executives make value decisions while their technical staff contributes to the rational aspect of the decision-making process. Note that both technical and value-based input can be used in a decision. I've applied decision analysis techniques in many decision situations because this method allows you to explicitly address both the technical issues and the values of the stakeholders (decision-makers).

4. **Analytics**: Finally, we can make decisions based on analytical tools and techniques (e.g., models). Models can be fact-based or values-based.

We have discussed a lot of information about solving problems, and while some of it may sound a little foreign, remember that you already use most (or all) of these steps when you make decisions. The difference now is that we're thinking about them so we can improve how we use these tools.

The last part of this problem solving discussion involves how the decision gets made. You'll probably find these very familiar too, when you pause to consider them.

When we attempt to make a decision, we can take a rather simplistic approach if the decision is straightforward. We don't need to overcomplicate a decision problem unless it is deserved! Here are three ways to make a decision when the situation is not complex. These rules require you to specify decision criteria or attributes for each alternative.

1. **Domination**: You can quickly reduce the number of alternative solutions by selecting the most important issue surrounding the problem and selecting the alternative that best meets this issue/objective/criterion. Note that some decisions cannot be made properly if you quickly eliminate other key issues. Also, note that if there are three important issues, and the same alternative dominates on all of the criteria, you've made a sound decision.

   For example, you are considering the purchase of a new car. Your most important criterion is price. You set the maximum price you are willing to pay. That decision criterion eliminates all options (cars) with prices above this threshold.

2. **Elimination**: In this rule, set a threshold of acceptance for a range of issues or criteria, and then eliminate alternatives that don't fall above the threshold. Note that this method does not recognize that some issues may be more important than others.

   Going back to the car example, now you want to base your decision on three variables, or criteria: cost, miles per gallon, and number of doors. If you were looking at four cars, and only one of them met your limits on cost, mpg, and number of doors, you are done. Note, for example, that with this method you're treating the importance of the number of doors equal to the importance of cost. This may not be the best tool to solve this particular problem.

3. **Lexicographic**: First, rank the decision criteria by importance. Then, take the most important criterion and apply it to the alternatives. The best one wins. If there is a tie, or it is close, go to the second-most important criterion and repeat.

   Continuing the previous example, let's say you rank cost higher than mpg or number of doors. You discover that two of your car options come in below your cost limit. Now compare the two cars against the second-most important criterion, mpg. If both cars fall above the mpg limit, go to the third criterion and see if both cars meet the number of doors criterion. This is an easy elimination process that can be useful for simple decisions or decisions where the criteria are very specific.

   Some decision situations are too complex for these basic approaches to decision-making. There are a number of decision tools that can be applied, depending upon the nature of the decision problem. Examples include pairwise comparison (an effective way to reduce a large number of options to a smaller number), decision tees, decision analysis, and analytical models. These methods are beyond the scope of this book. However, we do cover them in other educational materials. You'll find them at www.successfulconsultanttraining. com.

We will introduce one other decision tool that I've found to be quite useful in group settings. For example, you may be in a meeting with your client's staff, and you must facilitate a decision. The method we describe here, while basic in scope, can be effective.

I call this method Problem Option Solution, or the POS method. I learned this process from consultant Mel Hensey. Essentially, you take the group through three steps: discuss the problem, develop solution options, and select a solution together.

The first step is P, the Problem: State the problem context and its causes, in as much detail as possible or is known. State the facts, causes, and symptoms. Get everything out. Write what you get on a flip chart for all to see.

Next, go to O, the Options. Now ask the group to offer ideas for alternatives, or solution ideas. Any ideas, even apparently *outrageous* ones, are OK. No personal attacks are allowed, like "now that is a stupid idea, it will never work". Once again, write down all of the ideas on a flip chart and put it on the wall for all to see.

Finally, go to S, the Solution. Either go around the room and ask each person to suggest a solution (stressful on the shy), or just let anyone share (which usually means poor balance of participation). Either way is OK, although I prefer to put people on the spot rather than letting them sleep. Try telling the group that everyone needs to suggest something, and ask for volunteers first, so the shy people will have a little time to prepare themselves. Alternately, you can start with the shy people so they can present the more obvious solutions first. Record every idea or solution in the speaker's words on a flipchart. Now rank the ideas using the n/3 voting procedure (give attendees n/3 votes, where n = number of potential solutions you gathered). For example, if you wrote down nine possible solutions, then each person can vote for the 3 solutions they think are the best. The solution with the highest number of votes is ranked first, and so on for all of the solution alternatives.

If there are a lot of solutions, try taking a subset of the results and going through the process once more. So, if you had twelve solutions in the first round, take the top six for the second round and repeat the process, giving each person two votes. Finally, ask the group to help define an implementation plan.

This remarkably simple procedure is a great way to establish a consensus solution. It is particularly useful when working on annual plans for the firm, or a marketing strategy.

Finally, there are a number of ways decisions can be made when the basis is cost. You may be evaluating three different projects, and the goal is to select the project with the least cost. The simplest method is called the payback period. The payback period is the number of years required for a firm to recover its initial investment from the project's cash flows.

The insert shows two examples. In Example 1, two projects are being considered, with a project cost of $1,000. The payback period for Project A is 3 years, and the payback period for Project B is 5 years.

Payback Period Examples: Net Cash Flow

Example 1: Cost = $1000			Example 2: Cost = $600		
Year	A	B	Year	A	B
1	$500	$100	1	$200	$100
2	$300	$150	2	$150	$100
3	$200	$200	3	$150	$200
4	$400	$250	4	$100	$200
5		$300			
6		$350			

Because of its simplicity, the use of payback period can result in misleading conclusions. First, payback period ignores the income that occurs after the payback period. If the project matures much later, the decision may not be appropriate. Payback period also doesn't take into consideration the time value of money. For example, look at Example 2. Each project has a 6-year payback. However, we know that a dollar today is worth more than a dollar next year, so Project C, with a faster cash flow, is more attractive than Project D.

Finally, payback period emphasizes short-term effects on earnings. This may not maximize return in the long run.

Another useful measure is discounted cash flow, or the DCF Method. One variation of the DCF Method is called net present value (NPV). Net present value is the sum of all future cash flows, both inflows and outflows, adjusted for the time value of money (that is, the value of cash today is more valuable than cash at some point in the future).

In other words, you find the present value of the net cash flows through the years, discount them at the cost of capital, and subtract from the original project investment cost. If the NPV is positive, the project is viewed as attractive; conversely, if the NPV is negative, the project should be declined. Microsoft Excel has a good NPV calculator.

Yes, I know this has been a long, and sometime arduous, chapter. Take a break and proceed to your Success Roadmap and complete Section 10, Problem Assessment Template, and Section 11, Solution Selection. Then we'll finish this chapter with a discussion on risk management.

Risk Management

Our last topic in problem solving is risk management. Most problem situations involve some amount of risk, and a decision must be made regarding the level of risk that is acceptable, or some action is indicated to reduce the risk in some way. The purpose of risk management is to reduce the exposure to risks.

Business Risk is the exposure to unanticipated events that could negatively impact a project. Usually that risk is reflected in either increased cost or longer development timeframes, or both.

More specifically,

Business Risk = f (likelihood of the event times the magnitude of the consequences)

An event may pose a high risk because of a high probability of occurrence and high potential consequence, but we must be especially careful of risk events with a very low probability but very high consequences. An example is grain elevator dust explosions. If grain dust in a storage elevator reaches about 50 grams/cubic meter, with oxygen present in a contained space, and an ignition source occurs, a powerful explosion can take place that destroys the elevator and its contents. This is an example of a high consequence event with a low probability. When there is an unacceptable risk, the risk must be mitigated. Examples of risk mitigation for the grain elevator could include pneumatic dust control, liquid (water or oil) additives.

There are many kinds of business risks. Here are six common business risks:

1. **Cost risk**: This is probably the most common type of business risk. Cost risk is always a consideration for acquisitions, mergers, or the development of new projects or technologies. The acquirer or investor wants to know what potential liabilities there are, their consequences, and the likelihood of occurrence.

2. **Schedule risk**: Schedule risk often comes up when permitting or developing a new project.

A proxy for schedule risk is probability of delay, which can affect the development success of a project.

3. **Performance risk**: Performance risk typically deals with work quality. Another application is the performance of a new facility. Will the facility meet the performance standards?

4. **Regulatory risk**: This arises when a state legislature or Congress enacts a new bill that restricts commerce, or creates new taxes.

5. **Market risk**: An example of market risk is roll out of a new product. How will the consumer, or businesses, react to the product? Another market risk is the probability that a certain bond or stock continues to rise.

6. **Hazard risk**: Hazard risk includes seismic risk, weather risk (hurricanes, earthquakes), or upsets in manufacturing plants.

Consultants must be able to recognize forms of business risk so they can be in a position to help their clients.

Managing risk can be viewed as a three-step process: risk criteria development, risk analysis, and risk reduction. Let's take a quick look at these steps.

Step 1: **Risk Criteria Development**. The first step is to develop the risk criteria, or measures, that will be used to determine whether risks are acceptable. For example, if a firm is considering an acquisition, they may put a limit on the environmental liabilities, say $1,000,000. As they consider acquisitions, they would estimate the environmental liabilities for each.

Identifying criteria early will help direct your analysis. As you proceed with your analysis, your criteria definitions will change.

Step 2: **Risk Analysis.** The process of risk analysis involves identifying potential risk events (e.g., oil spill from a utility transformer leak), estimating the likelihood that each event could occur, estimating the consequences of the event (e.g., soil contamination), and estimating the cost of the event (e.g., clean the soil).

Step 3: **Risk Reduction Strategies.** If a risk analysis indicates that the estimated risks are significant, then efforts will be made to mitigate the risk. The primary strategies, based upon the likelihood of occurrence and severity of the consequences of the risk event, are:

▶ Risk reduction,

▶ Risk transfer, and

▶ Risk acceptance.

Under risk reduction, you can either reduce the likelihood of occurrence of the risk, or you can reduce the consequence of a risk event. For example, installing a groundwater monitoring system under an underground tank will reduce the consequences of a release. Installing a double-walled tank will reduce the likelihood of a release. Note that reducing the likelihood of occurrence is typically the more difficult task because it may require a costly change in technology.

Risk transfer can be accomplished either by transferring the risk to an insurance company (a common practice),

Risk Management Strategies

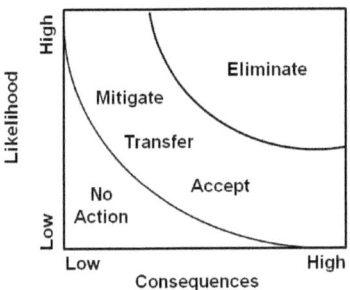

or by selling the division that has the risk to another firm.

And finally, you can simply accept the risk if the risk cost is reasonable and insurable (for example, through pollution liability insurance for an underground tank).

5. Client Service for Consultants

C lient service means doing everything one possibly can to continuously build a client relationship and put in the foundation for a steady increase

Profit in business comes from repeat customers; customers that boast about your product and service, and that bring friends with them.
—W. Edwards Deming

the revenues client relationship and put in the foundation for a steady increase in revenues from that client. There are many things you can do to achieve this goal. I'm going to share some of my most effective tools in this chapter.

The first step toward great client service is to create recognition so that they listen to you. Prospects and clients must know your name. Well, that sounds obvious, right? *Duh!*

What I really mean, however, is that you must keep your name in front of your prospects and existing clients. For example, send frequent emails with valuable information. This could be something as simple as a summary of relevant news items you found on the Internet. Remember, your client may not be spending time looking for events or other news in their field, and they may appreciate a reminder about an important conference or news item.

A number of years ago, while working at a consulting firm, we were struggling to win work in the waste remediation field. One of my senior managers started sending a monthly newsletter to all of the electric utility companies within 100 miles of our office. Within 6 months, we had a remediation practice and after 18 months, we had one of the largest practices in the northeast.

Your prospect or client needs to be able to find you. Now that one sounds obvious, too! But what I mean here is that you must make it easy and you must be available almost all of the time. Provide your office phone, cell phone, email, mailing address, and tell your client to call anytime, and emphasize the word "anytime". One time we were working with a firm that experienced a real regulatory compliance problem that could result in some bad publicity. It was Thanksgiving Day eve, around 6 PM. The client was looking for a solution to be delivered on Friday morning after Thanksgiving. We worked all Thanksgiving Day. That client quickly became our best and largest client for the next several years. (I'm not trying to scare you away from consulting with that story, but it's worth knowing up front that if an emergency happens, you could lose time you once considered sacrosanct. The consultant who can provide results between close of business Friday and 8 AM Monday morning—or the morning after Thanksgiving—is the consultant whose clients will trust him or her to get the job done. That's the consultant your client will think of first when a problem occurs, and you want that consultant to be you!

What Clients Want from You

It is important to know what prospects and clients want from their consultants, in addition to excellent work at a reasonable price. What follows is a description of ten things that my clients have consistently wanted to see from their consultants. See how many of these you can provide!

1. **Change**: Clients want change… that is why they need help. You must show how you will bring change. This is why you are being engaged by the client. Change means improvement over the current state. How will you change the current situation and improve the client's results? These could be long-term results (structural, corporate-level) or short-term results (getting your client's deliverable finished on time when they couldn't have achieved that without your services).

2. **Cutting Edge**: Clients want the latest technology or the best and brightest ideas. This is critically important. Clients expect that you will have the latest and greatest. Package your service in a way that infers that you are at the cutting edge of your field. Research the latest innovations in your field, and include at least one new idea, and mention this in your marketing. Even if you are using "tried and true" techniques, there is a way you can present your work that appears to be cutting edge. Now, if you are truly challenged on this one, try including a case history or two where other clients have used your techniques.

3. **Perspective**: Your client wants to know what his/her peers are doing and what agency regulations are on the horizon. They want to know the "big

picture". Once again, do your research and be aware of what is going on in the client's market. What are your client's competitors or peers doing that your client should be doing? In my experience, clients expect that you are aware of their market, and they expect that you will share your experiences with them. Remember, "keeping up with the Joneses" is a powerful driving force for people, including your prospects and clients!

4. **Functionality**: Show the client how your solution will work or how it will be used. They want to know *how* it is going to solve their problem. Functionality also means flexibility. Show that your approach to providing a service is flexible, so that you can accommodate unanticipated events.

5. **Brand**: You need a brand that the client will recognize. For example, I am recognized as a siting expert; others are recognized as regulatory experts, wetlands experts, hydrogeology experts, or project managers; still others are recognized simply as organized, or schedule-driven, or able to get a project back on schedule... and so on. Position yourself to be a brand. Brand all of your marketing materials and your website. Try writing a personal brand statement, and use it in your marketing material. This statement should be a paragraph in length and address what attributes set you apart, what audience you serve, what you do, and why you do it. Your brand is a powerful tool that can increase trust and credibility. (Pause and take a shot at this paragraph right now, or consider the answers you wrote down in Step 7 in your Roadmap to Success.)

6. **One-stop**: Clients want one-stop shopping, and do not want to hire several consultants to solve what they see as one problem. That doesn't mean you have to be an expert in everything! If needed, create a team to solve the client's problem. Bring in other consultants that you know or who are recommended by people you know. I have been in this situation often. I get a potential client interested in my service, but then the client adds other tasks to the scope. I go out and get other experts to address these issues for me. I subcontract those experts, and I manage them so my client doesn't have to. You can do the same.

7. **Commonality**: Your client wants to see that you understand their situation, speak their lingo. How does this happen? By getting to know your client from a personal perspective. Or, when you first enter a client's office, look around. What is hanging on the wall? What pictures are on the desk? What awards are framed? Look for something to comment on and create some commonality. I was introduced to a prospect awhile back, and I thought it would be difficult getting to know him because I was in a geographic location unfamiliar to me, and his interests appeared so different from mine. However, he mentioned that he'd been part of a new business enterprise many years ago. It turned out that I had been as well! From there on, our relationship flourished.

8. **Show the Future**: Clients want to know what the future looks like when your solution is implemented. *Consultants* seem to focus only on *their* solution... how and why it works. Take another

step and describe what your client's future will look like *after* your solution is implemented. Clients are impressed when you predict the future in a confident manner. In my site selection practice, I often create a proposal cover showing a site with a new facility, thus showing the client what his future would look like—his fully developed project!

9. **Value Pricing**: Clients want to know they are getting good value. Demonstrate extreme value or use

---

There is only one boss. The customer. And he can fire everybody in the company from the chairman on down, simply by spending his money somewhere else.
—Sam Walton, Founder of Wal-Mart

---

comparison pricing to put your offer in perspective. Or, show the client how you are saving them money, time, or even better, *both*! How would your service increase their profit or put them at an advantage to their competitors?

10. **Leadership**: Clients are looking to be led. What does this mean? What does it mean to be led by a consultant? First, a consultant-leader stands up for what he believes is right for the client. Second, he isn't afraid to challenge the status quo and suggest new ideas. Third, he is willing to recognize other good ideas, especially the client's good ideas.

Once again, take time to examine each of these ten issues or factors. Every one of them is important, and if you specifically address all of them, you will be surprised at the reception you get from your clients!

Client Expectations

It is critically important to create an atmosphere where you always meet, and often exceed, the expectations of your clients. Exceeding expectations is one of the most powerful relationship-building factors.

Communicate frequently with your clients. This is the best way to understand what your client expects from you.

This insert shows the Client Expectations Pyramid, with five levels of client expectations. The lowest level is a place you never want to visit: dissatisfaction. It's actually *beneath* the pyramid. When you reside there, as shown to the right of the pyramid, you tend to lose clients, or at least you lose future opportunities with the client.

The next higher level is Base Expectations. These expectations are implicit, in that clients don't talk about them; they are in the background, but they are very important. You *must* meet the basic expectations. Examples of basic expectations are showing interest in the client, communicating on a regular basis, producing documents that have a professional appearance and are readable (no typos, understandable, logical, etc.).

The next higher level is called Requirements, which are explicit, such as the instructions contained in a Request for Proposal. If you are able to follow instructions, and meet the base expectations, you will stay in the game, continue to get on bidders' lists, and receive opportunities. And, *you may get some work.* If you choose not to follow the instructions in a Request for Proposal, ask yourself why. Until you get your proposal to your client, you have little hope of a job opportunity. And if you don't follow the guidance in a Request for Proposal, how can your potential client expect that you will be able to follow much more complex instructions related to the job you're after?

After the Requirements level comes the Unexpected level, where you step out of the box and offer a service that goes beyond that requested. The Unexpected level is latent, in that you offer something that is hidden from other proposers, something that is distinctly yours. Now you are positioning yourself to get sole-source work (a relationship with your client where they don't shop around for work you can provide, but always come directly to you). You may also receive more add-ons to your existing contracts. However, there is one more level to strive for!

Delight is the highest expectations level. At this level, you have *truly* earned the trust of the client and he expects only the best ideas and solutions from you. He may be willing to elevate the relationship to that of a partner or alliance partner. Or, you may be able to execute a Master Contract that opens up many more opportunities for you. And stepping aside from the purely monetary part of consulting, it feels fantastic to so successfully satisfy my clients; I'm telling you this from personal experience.

As a consultant, you must constantly assess where you are on this pyramid. It is OK to start by meeting base expectations and work your way to the top.

It is not automatic. It takes persistent effort. However, it will be worth it.

Client Feedback

Nothing will help you advance your client relationships like asking for and responding to client feedback. However, few consultants really do this, and many who do mishandle the effort so badly that it hurts more than helps. Why is this? Well, it is likely because we don't want to hear bad news.

It's tough for many of us to ask for feedback because we don't want to hear about problems, especially problems that involve us!

> *Feedback is the breakfast of champions.*
> *—Ken Blanchard*

A couple of years ago, I engaged a large consulting firm to help me do some air quality permitting work. After they completed the work, I received a call from their project manager, who asked if I would take some time to provide feedback. Initially, I was impressed with the invitation. I said sure I would! The next day I received an email with five very simple questions. It was a canned feedback form! I felt insulted. There was nothing specific about my project, and I felt that I was sending a response into a black hole.

Client feedback must be carried out live, and preferably in person. This process is simply too important for anything less. A few years ago, I was asked by another office in the consulting firm where I was working to go to one of their clients, whose headquarters was close to my office. I asked the office about the type of work they were doing, and then held the meeting. The client was impressed that we would send someone to them just to receive feedback! They wouldn't stop talking. At the end of the meeting I asked if there were more work opportunities ahead for our firm.

They responded in the affirmative, and our work with that firm expanded by 50% in the next twelve months.

Note how we conducted the feedback. We did not send the project manager. I was an objective listener. The client was free to be honest and frank about the work, including the performance of the project manager, who is a critical part of the project. If you are an independent consultant, do the feedback meeting yourself. Don't worry about the objective listener. But be prepared to *welcome* criticism. I'm very serious about this; if your client offers you a criticism, *thank him or her.* Your client is giving you a gift; he or she is letting you know an area in which you can improve, so you can better serve that client and others—and earn more work! Whatever you do, don't argue with your client or try to justify yourself. The client is doing you a favor by offering you feedback that will help you both. If you reject something they're offering, you're pretty much ending the feedback opportunity and potentially offending your client.

> *The single biggest problem in communication is the illusion that it has taken place.*
>
> —*George Bernard Shaw*

The key to getting useful feedback from clients is to ask the right questions. Here are a few questions you should consider asking.

1. "What do you like best about working with us?" This is a good opening question because it gets you off to a positive start.

2. "What is the most disappointing experience you've had with us in the past year?" Ask this later in the interview *after* a few positive questions.

3. "What can we change about your relationship with us to make it more effective for you?" A great question.

4. "If you have a problem with our firm, do you know who to contact?" It is very important for the client to know who they should contact.

5. "Are our rates in line with the value we provide?" This is a super question! It indirectly asks how you are doing versus your competition.

6. "Are there any issues that you want to discuss about our performance?" Nice open-ended question.

7. "Where do you see the market in the next year or so?" An essential question to learn about the client's future plans and uncover any new opportunities.

8. "What opportunities do you see for us in the future?" Always end with this kind of question. Take this opportunity to learn about the client's current and future needs—and to put you in their mind as the possible solution to them.

Client Communication

Clearly, how you communicate with your clients is important. Always have a goal for the communication, and decide how you will communicate to achieve that goal. Peter Senge's *The Fifth Discipline Handbook* provides an excellent analysis of how we communicate. In general, there are three types of communication goals:

▶ **Exploration**: In this communication mode, the goal is to collect information and/or learn about a particular subject. No decision is needed.

> *The most important thing in communication is to hear what isn't being said.*
>
> —*Peter Drucker*

▶ **Consensus**: In this communication mode, the objective is to achieve a consensus decision.

▶ **Advocacy**: In this communication mode, you are taking a stand and advocating your position. This mode is used by many people in many settings; however, it may not be appropriate for most client-consultant communication.

Let's discuss each of these modes. The first mode is *exploration*. We seek to have a dialogue, and we allow each member of a group equal time to speak. Interrupting is forbidden. Listening is active… that is, we suspend our assumptions and opinions. There is no drive toward a consensus—just a dialogue. There is no attempt to make a decision, and no attempt to stake out a position.

The emphasis is on learning and discovery. Everyone contributes. If there is disagreement, this is reason for digging deeper. Exploration, then, is used when you need to collect information in an unbiased environment.

The next communication mode is *consensus seeking*. We use this mode when the purpose is to work toward closure, or converge on a decision. This mode requires that an agenda be in place. Team members accept priorities and assignments. Agreed upon meeting protocols are followed.

Members must be willing to be influenced by other team members. This is a key requirement. While there is advocacy of positions, there also is time for inquiry, or exploration, to expose positions. When an impasse occurs, the question must be asked: "How do we move forward?" What are the facts around the impasse, and what are the key concerns and the values behind the concerns?

Unnecessary confrontations can sometimes be avoided by listening first, then rephrasing, before responding. For example, "So what I think you said is X. Is that correct?" If you misunderstood, then the need for confrontation evaporates. If you did understand, you've given yourself and your listener a moment before challenging them. Note that meetings with a consensus-building objective must be led; they don't happen by accident!

Finally, we have the *advocacy* mode. Advocacy is equivalent to a debate, where views are presented and defended. We search for the "best" position or view. Each of the team members heave ideas or views at each other. The advantage of advocacy is that the person who believes most strongly in his or her view typically wins. The disadvantage is... that the person who believes most strongly in his or her view typically wins!

Unfortunately, in an advocacy atmosphere, learning is undermined. You are concentrating on attack and defense rather than learning or exploring, and when we are committed to a specific point of view, we're reluctant to hear any information that confronts it. (Think of political factions in an election year; plenty of people are talking, but very few are listening.) This mode of conversation is typical in most situations. We are used to stating a position and defending it. As consultants, however, we need to think about those political factions and consider whether anyone who doesn't already agree with the advocate is really going to listen to what's being so strongly pushed.

We need to realize the limitations to communicating in this manner.

Suggested Meeting Ground Rules

► Be additive, not repetitive
► Participate fully – take risks
► Avoid interruptions
► Be willing to be influenced
► Don't be a time hog
► Don't personalize disagreement
► No sidebars!
► No texting!

For example, advocacy tends to build a competitive relationship between group members, which may not be constructive. Be careful when you advocate in a client setting. *Remember, the best consultant position is facilitating.*

Always think about which communication mode is best applied in a client meeting, and apply that mode in your meeting. You will notice the difference!

<u>Running Effective Meetings</u>

A related topic is running effective meetings with your clients. Here are my ten guidelines for running great meetings:

1. Read, post, or distribute meeting ground rules. It is always helpful to remind attendees of these meeting rules.

2. Always ensure that there is a clear purpose, and clear desired result. Ensure that all attendees understand the purpose.

3. Ask the team members to suggest changes to the agenda and approve the agenda.

4. Assign member roles: facilitator, recorder, and timekeeper. The facilitator, often the team leader, controls the meeting in terms of who has the floor

and following the agenda. The recorder takes notes and distributes the notes after the meeting. The timekeeper reminds the facilitator if the meeting goes off schedule.

5. At the conclusion of the meeting, have a meeting critique. How can the meeting process be improved the next time?

6. Schedule the next meeting before adjourning.

7. Assign homework to be prepared by the attendees before the next meeting.

8. Quickly copy and distribute the meeting notes.

9. Using old-fashioned flipcharts to record meeting work is always helpful. Post each page on a wall as it is completed. This way, the entire meeting memory is available to the team. (These days, some recorders snap pictures of the flip chart pages with their smart phones and distribute them with the meeting notes.)

10. Use a "parking lot" to record issues that should be considered, but are not on this meeting's agenda. Revisit the "parking lot" at the end of the meeting to see what may need to be assigned or included on the next meeting's agenda.

OK, time to take a break and complete Section 12, Client Relationship Plan, in your Success Roadmap. Then we will discuss project management.

Project Management

Project management is a critical function for project managers because a client can easily see the results. Solid project management shows, just like poor project management. Furthermore, stellar project management is akin to good marketing, in that it leads to more work. That's why project management is included in the Client Service chapter

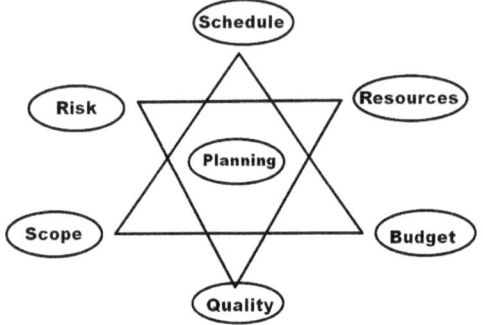

Project Management Double Triangle

Schedule

Risk

Resources

Planning

Scope

Budget

Quality

Let's begin by listing a few common problems that will not endear you to your client:

▶ **Poor communication** almost always leads to problems. Projects will gradually come off the tracks without at least weekly (several times per week for large or complex projects) calls or meetings.

▶ **Making decisions without the facts** creates problems. Before making decisions, make sure that you have *all* of the facts. Clients don't like consultants who have trigger fingers.

▶ **Hiding problems** never helps your client—or you. If you detect a problem on your project, bring it to the attention of your client immediately, even if you firmly believe the problem can be solved uneventfully. This will signal the client that you are looking out for their interests.

▶ **Starting a project without a meeting of the minds** between you and the client regarding the work scope. Don't just rely on the scope contained in the proposal. Create a new scope document and get the client's approval before you begin work. This protects both you and your client, and makes you better able to stay near the top of that client expectations pyramid we discussed earlier.

▶ **Scope creep.** Even if the term is new to you, most of your clients will be far too familiar with it. Scope creep, put simply, is the expansion of required tasks outside the contracted scope of work you made with your client. Scope creep usually costs your client more money. If the client requests additional work, provide a change of scope (written notice of the client's request and your acceptance of the additional work—and additional charges) as soon as possible. If you realize that additional work you didn't already scope needs to be performed, let the client know. (Even if you decide not to charge for the extra work—maybe especially if you decide not to charge for it—the sooner the client knows, the lower the risk that they'll be dissatisfied by your bill.)

▶ **Starting a project without a specific, defined deliverable.** When you begin a project, write down the specific deliverable expected by the client. Then create one or more metrics that will enable you to closely track progress against this deliverable. The metrics should include schedule, cost, and tracking work progress versus expenditures (this will enable you to detect budget problems early).

▶ **Not identifying risks.** Another useful activity at the start of a project is to create a "risk register", or listing of the possible project risks that could affect your project in terms of cost, schedule, or work quality. For example, if opposition could impact permit schedules, include a work task to monitor potential project opposition to anticipate intervention.

Project management consists of seven key tasks, often termed the project management double triangle, shown in the insert.

All projects should begin with planning. The purpose of planning is to ensure that the project moves forward in concert with the contract and approved work scope. Don't assume that the scope contained in the proposal is correct. A Project Management Plan (PMP) should be prepared that lays out all of the key issues at the start, including the work scope, contract, communication protocols, schedule, and billing. The PMP ensures that you begin the project on the same wavelength as your client.

Gantt Chart

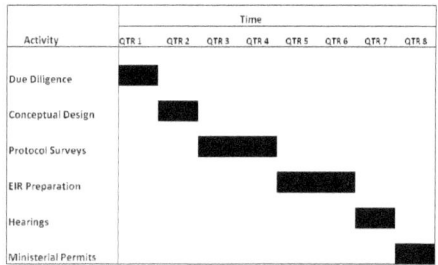

Resource procurement and management is essential. The project manager must assign sufficient staff (the *right* staff) to complete the project within the cost and schedule constraints. The project manager should create a "mini-contract" with each team member in which the team member agrees to prepare the deliverable at a pre-approved budget. When you do this, team members are held accountable for any budget overruns (at the very least the office must write down the overruns in this case).

Tracking project progress using a scheduling system is critical. Depending upon the nature and complexity of the project, milestones or a simple Gantt chart may be sufficient. Or, the project may require a program such as Microsoft Project (whose default display is very similar to a Gantt chart, but the software does much of the scheduling work automatically).

Budget tracking is another essential task. Typically, a spreadsheet is used to track expenditures. Most consulting firms use standard accounting software that provides weekly updates of budget performance. If that isn't available, use an Excel spreadsheet. Remember too that you're only worried about the budget you're responsible for; if it's just you and your company's team, you only need to track your company's budget. If you've been tasked with managing your client's project budget, make sure you're familiar with the accounting software they use, or that you have a proficient administrative staffer within the client's company who will assist you in this task.

We discussed project risks earlier. Always spend the effort to understand where the project could go awry, and create mitigation plans if needed. All too often, consultants don't plan ahead for possible risk events. Clients become surprised and disappointed. By the way, this is a great example of proactive problem finding!

Ensuring project work quality is another important function of the project manager. Typically, the project manager engages a peer reviewer, who has the responsibility of reviewing all work products before they are sent to the client for their review. Before starting a project, learn about your client's view of work quality. For example, I've had several clients who interpreted a draft report as final, and would not tolerate any typos in the draft. If you don't have a peer reviewer, budget for and then hire a professional to review your documents before submitting them.

Now it is time to create your own Project Management Plan template. Complete Section 13 in the Success Roadmap. Then it is onto the final chapter, Business Planning, the foundation of your business.

6. Business Planning for Consultants

The first task for a new consultancy is to create a plan. However, I positioned this chapter near the end of this book because I wanted you to understand the key aspects of consulting before discussing planning.

Over the years, I've found that planning is one of the most difficult tasks to teach consultants to do. Moreover, and admittedly, planning has been a chore for me as well! My take on this is that planning is mostly an individual, and personal, activity, as opposed to writing a report, for example, which tends to be better defined, and will be submitted to a client.

> *"The plan is useless; it's the planning that is important."*
>
> —*Dwight D. Eisenhower*

In addition, many people simply don't believe that thinking ahead accomplishes anything worthwhile. However, based on my experience, planning *is* worthwhile, and if conducted properly, will improve how you will conduct your work (and will either save you time, earn you more money, or both).

The best example I have is to consider your revenue goal for the next year. Let's assume that you determined that

$80,000 is required to pay your bills, and provide sufficient funds for other purposes. Also, let's assume that you left your former job and want to start a consultancy. Your task is to think through how you will earn $80,000 in the next twelve months. That will be a challenge for you, and you will be forced to "think out of the box" as to how much you should charge for your services and how you will win enough clients and jobs to reach $80,000. If you did not give this some serious thought and work up a solid plan of action, your chances of meeting the $80,000 goal would be small.

In summary, the value to planning and goal setting is that it will alter how you think about your future. You will gain insights into what level of effort and what actions will be required to meet your goals.

In this chapter, we will cover the following planning topics:

▶ Overall Business Goals
▶ Marketing Plan
▶ Sales Plan
▶ Operations Plan
▶ Legal and Risk Plan
▶ Financial Plan
▶ Billing Rates

Note that we have addressed some of these topics already. However, I think that putting them in one place will help you see the "big picture" here. Also, I am adding new material for each topic, so it isn't just a review.

Business Goals

When thinking about your business goals for the next year, everything should start with your profit goal if you are, or want to be, an independent consultant. Of course, a revenue goal will be more relevant to you (as an independent consultant, most of your expenses are paid, so your personal expenses are relatively low). Then you create the links between revenue and the actions you must undertake to reach that revenue goal.

Backing up a bit, how do you determine your revenue goal? Start with what you really want out of your new career (consulting, freelancing, contracting, etc.). Try to answer these questions:

▶ What kind of home do you want?
▶ Where do you want to live?
▶ What overhead will you have to pay yourself that you didn't as an employee (health insurance, unemployment insurance, fees for professionals such as tax preparers, etc.)?
▶ What expenses do you expect for your children (education, etc.)?
▶ What types of vacations do you like?

In other words, create you lifestyle (with some reason!).

Then estimate the monthly or annual income you need to support this lifestyle. Add some expenses, and you have your revenue goal. I suggested some potential expenses for you to take into account on the first page of Chapter 2. Review that information now if you have any questions.

Marketing Plan

The most important plan you will make is the marketing plan. Marketing is the engine of growth in your venture. However, as stated by none other than Dwight Eisenhower, the plan itself is useless. It is the thinking behind the plan that is important.

Most consultants bypass the marketing plan and go straight to marketing. Results may be achieved with this approach, but it is very unlikely that this approach will be optimal. Once again, the purpose of planning is to shape the future, or, in other words, create a future of higher revenues, a better work schedule, or other issues related to your values.

Before proceeding, I think it's important remind you of the value of adopting a marketing system. Employing a system enables you to track results and learn what works and what doesn't work. In other words, you get more of what you measure, and *you learn as you carry out your marketing.* Learning leads to better results.

Tracking also takes the emotion out of it. Maybe you think, "I haven't accomplished anything!" Reviewing your tracking system will prove you wrong (or right, which tells you where you need to improve); it will show you how many calls, emails, client meetings, proposals, and jobs you've gotten. Objective information trumps negative emotions almost every time.

Let's get started. If you'd like to take a break and revisit your marketing plan in your Success Roadmap, feel free—and keep your notebook handy as you read this chapter

When I embark upon the task of creating a marketing plan, I typically perform the following steps:

- ▶ Describe the Objectives
- ▶ Describe Your Service and Develop Your Compelling Marketing Message
- ▶ Identify Your Customer Profile

> ▶ Examine the Macro-environment
> ▶ Create a Lead Generation Strategy, and
> ▶ Adopt a Budget and Metrics

The objective of the marketing plan should be a metric that reflects a result you're looking for, such as number of new clients needed in the next year (based upon your estimate of the revenue per client), or the revenue expected from your key clients, if you already have clients. These assumptions should be based upon some data collected regarding these clients or potential clients.

Next, what is the service that will be offered? You can review Section 6 from your Roadmap to Success notebook, where you detailed your offering. For your marketing plan, you're aiming for a summary of the most important elements. How does the service help your customers? Does the service have a name? How does the service work? What is the worth of the service to a customer? What does the service cost?

How do you want to approach your market? For example, you can market by industry, where you approach every company in that industry, such as chemical companies. The advantage here is that you can easily leverage your experience. Or, you can simply target the companies you think match up best with your offering. Third, you can target companies (in different sectors) who may need your service. here, you lose the ability to apply much of what you learn from Company A and apply it to Company B in the same industry. Let's assume you choose to market by industry sector.

With a firm understanding of your service, decide which market segments you will target, or, in other words, who is your ideal customer? Be as specific as possible. For example, if you wanted to market to the electric utility industry sector,

Market Sector Selection Strategy

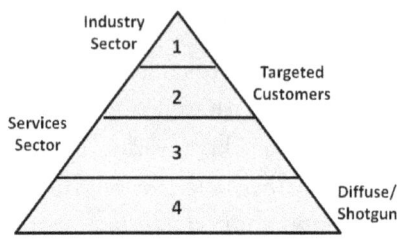

do you want to talk to all utilities? Do you want to sell to utilities that specialize in coal generation, gas-fired generation, hydro-electric generation, nuclear generation, or renewables? If you want to sell to firms generating renewable energy, do you want to work in wind power or solar power or biomass power? If you select solar power, do you wish to focus on thermal solar or photovoltaic solar? If you selected thermal, do you want to focus on power towers, parabolic mirror technologies, or dish technologies? You can see that we can drill down to a much smaller, better-focused market segment. Since you're aiming for mastery of your discipline, being as specific as you can when defining your market helps guide your educational and business development as well.

Think about your market. Separate it into its segments and decide which segments will provide the best opportunity (i.e., segments where your service is most compatible or most needed).

Once you have your market segments selected, think about the needs of those segments. Start with the emotional needs (what do they need, what are they worried about?). What are the specific results your customers want? Do they want more money? Do they want a higher profit? What do they want to avoid? Do they want to avoid complying with a certain regulation? Do they want to be more secure? Do they want to avoid work overload? In other words, what are the key emotional motivators? These motivators will be more important than the non-emotional motivators, such as an analysis, a report, and so on.

Now that you understand your customer's key problem, what solution do you have to solve the problem? What is your unique sales proposition? Why is your solution better than the competition? Again, you've already identified some answers to these questions in your Roadmap to Success notebook.

Next, consider the macro-environment and how it may affect your customer's business. For example, are there any new regulations emerging that will hurt your customer? Perhaps your customer has 49 employees, and wants to avoid paying health insurance for his/her employees. Engaging consultants could help.

> *"People buy feelings. They buy piece of mind. Not services. Not products. Not knowledge. Not expertise."*
>
> Dan Kennedy

Are there any legislative incentives that could help your client? In the solar business, the federal government and some state governments offer grants and tax incentives for new solar projects. How about market trends? Is your client's business expected to expand or contract during the next few years? Does the answer offer any opportunity for you? Does the answer suggest that you should refocus your efforts on a different area of your field?

I'm going to use energy production as an example again. Solar and other renewable energy has great potential and is projected to expand dramatically over the next 20 years. On the other hand, after the Daiichi Nuclear Power Plant disaster, many countries have become leery of considering new nuclear facilities, and anti-nuclear organizations are fighting nuclear energy with renewed vigor. If your service could help both markets, the knowledge that renewables are expanding and nuclear is contracting could help you decide which market to target.

OK, with that rather long preamble, we're ready to get into the lead generation strategy. Lead generation, in my opinion, is the lifeblood of a consulting business. It is not great customer service. It is not your "leading" service or product. Once again, if you didn't get it the first time, *it is lead generation.*

Here are the most common lead generation techniques:

▶ **Directed Marketing/Networking**: This is a common, and perhaps the most effective, marketing method for consultants. Directed marketing means you target specific clients and individuals. They might be past clients, referrals, or targets of opportunity. Because most of these contacts already know you, are familiar with your business, and respect what you have accomplished, they will be the shortest path to initial success. *Make a note of the individuals you will contact directly.*

▶ **Conference Attendance/Present a Paper/Staff a Booth**: Conferences are terrific places to get leads for many services. There are hundreds of trade associations and other organizations that support a constituency. Investigate which conferences or meetings would offer excellent opportunities for lead generation. If it is too costly to attend, try purchasing the proceedings or joining a group booth. A terrific example of this is the National Association of Television Programming Executives (NATPE) Expo. Say you're a consultant for documentary filmmakers; the International

Documentary Association always buys a booth there. While buying your own booth might be cost-prohibitive, buying in—or volunteering—to the IDA's booth could get you to the event for a price you can afford. *Attend the conferences and/or other trade meetings, chamber meetings, etc. that can provide leads.*

▶ **Email Marketing**: Email marketing means sending regular emails (e.g., a newsletter or e-zine) to a list of your prospects and customers with the goal of expanding your relationship with them, and, ultimately, selling them your services. These emails, however, must provide value to your list. As we've discussed, value can be news or other developments important to your list, ideas for enhancing results, or simply a compilation of great ideas from other people or organizations.

Many email-based marketing programs also use a website. The emails drive traffic to the website, where you can provide more details about your service and make offers.

If you don't have a list for emailing, you may be able to rent email lists for your target audience. If you search the phrase "direct mail lists", you will find a number of firms that offer hundreds of email lists.

If you think email marketing can work for you, create a series of emails. Once again, a simple newsletter can be effective.

▶ **Direct Mail**: Direct mail is one of the best media for building long-term relationships. In the era of the Internet, many consultants ignore direct mail. However, as you can see in your mailbox, direct mail is still quite alive. Billions are being spent on direct mail advertising. The key advantages of direct mail include the ability to test what works and doesn't, and determine when the "open rate" is high. If your mail looks professional, it gets opened. That is usually a lot better than how most emails are treated. Another advantage is that there are thousands of lists that can be rented. Therefore, you can target very effectively. On the negative side, recent increases in postage have made direct mail a more expensive vehicle.

One alternative is to use postcards. Again, most people ignore this method. However, it is less expensive than mailing sales letters. In this case, you need to include a strong call to action and send the reader to a website, an email address, or phone number.

You can find lots of free or inexpensive lists out there. For example, I wanted to market to electric utility executives. I found a directory of utility personnel that included thousands of names. The directory cost $200. Direct mail is an established and successful marketing method. It is used by about 80% of companies who spend money on marketing. *Investigate the availability of lists that you can use. Try a small mailer, a letter or postcard, and evaluate the results.*

▶ **Advertise**: Advertising is another lead generation method that few consultants seem to utilize. However, it can be a good way to reach out to prospects and build a brand. I'm not talking about "general advertising" here. Rather, I'm talking about very focused advertising. For example, in the regular media, try small space ads in magazines that are read by your prospects. If your topic is starting a home business, advertise in magazines such as Home Business, Entrepreneur, or Inc. Place a small ad that briefly explains your service, and include a phone number as well as website and email addresses.

Another option is to advertise on the Internet, which we discussed in some detail in the last two sections of Chapter 3. You can purchase ads on Facebook, Yahoo, or LinkedIn, or purchase small banner ads on blog sites that are on your topic. Always test with small campaigns first.

The challenge with Internet marketing is that you must get the prospect to click, which sends them to your website or Facebook page, and then they need to opt-in. This two-step process can make your conversion rate very low. *Advertising can be a good way to build your brand; however, be careful about cost. Always try short-term ads and measure their response. Test different messages, images, formats, etc.*

▶ **Webinars/Seminars**: Seminars and webinars are great methods to build a consulting practice. Seminars can be given at a target company. Or, you can advertise and hold a seminar in a hotel conference room. Webinars are very popular now. Webinars use a service such as Go To Meeting, which provides a platform for the online meeting that includes both video (either of you speaking or of documents you wish to display that share your information) and audio. Webinars are ideally suited to Powerpoint presentations.

If you are selling your service on a webinar, start with a description of the key problem that your customers are facing. What are their emotional concerns? Add some data to support your contention that this problem is important. Show where other customers experienced the problem. Finally, offer your solution. *Seminars and webinars are perfect methods to sell your services. Look for opportunities to use these techniques in your marketing.*

▶ **Website** with Organic and/or Paid Traffic: More consultants are using a website to sell their services. Of course, sites like Elance and Vworker have thousands of freelancers selling their services. If you set up your own site, there are two broad ways to drive traffic to the site. The first is organic traffic (also called free traffic). There are many ways to drive traffic organically. A few of the more popular methods are "search engine optimization" (or SEO), writing articles that create links back to your site, posting articles or information about your service on social network sites like Facebook, posting Youtube videos that link back to your site, or posting information about your services on various blogs. Organic traffic is very dependent upon the use of the correct keywords; that is, the keywords that your prospects will use to find providers of your service.

▶ Paid traffic includes paying for ads on sites like Facebook, Yahoo, and LinkedIn. Facebook ads work best for sales to consumers, and LinkedIn ads work best in a business-to-business environment. These ads are comprised of a heading, body copy, and an image. Even small changes to these elements can make a giant difference in clicks. Therefore, to be successful with pay-per-click, you must test many versions of headlines, text, and images. Headlines must address key emotional motivations of the customer. Images of people often work better than pictures of things.

Make a strong call to action in the body text. Websites have become an attractive way to promote your business. You can drive ad traffic to the website.

We've discussed seven different marketing methods to obtain leads. Evaluate these methods and determine which ones would be most appropriate for your business. Write down specific goals for each method. For example, rent a list of 1,000 email addresses and send them a sales letter that directs them to a website. Attend a relevant meeting or conference and seek out at least ten leads. Spend $10 per ad and test 25 different Facebook ads. Use several lead generation methods. Each method will reach a different segment of your target audience.

Your marketing strategy is a critical step toward the success you desire. You must set goals to reach the results you need. Have you identified goals in your Success Roadmap?

Finally, develop a sales forecast and budget for your marketing, and track your results with a few metrics, such as conversion rate for Internet marketing, or number of new clients, revenue goals for existing clients, blog posts, web traffic, articles posted, meetings with prospects, etc.

Sales Plan and Proposal Template

A sales plan describes how you will win work from your qualified leads. The first step in sales is to build a good relationship with the leads. Gather intelligence as the relationship improves. Add value frequently by providing useful information, reports, news items, etc.

Most consulting assignments are won using some form of written proposal or presentation. Therefore, it is important to craft very good proposal and presentation templates so that you can prepare them quickly and still attain a high level of quality and effectiveness.

Work on the content and graphics now, when you have the time to get it right. Make the proposal document look professional. Adopt an attractive format. Make the document easy to read by using white space and images to break up the text. If you're using word processing software, apply styles so that, if the client requests a specific format (like a particular font or font size), you can make the change once rather than changing paragraphs or headings individually.

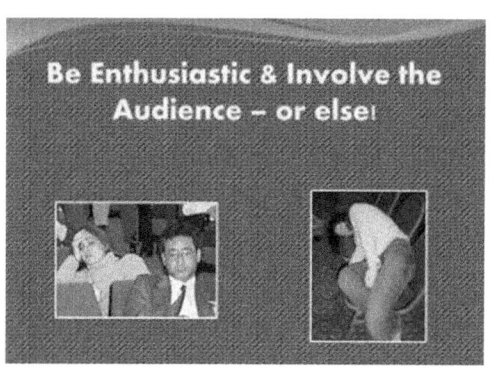

For presentations, get their attention at the start by doing something unexpected (e.g., use a prop, show a short video, try a brief demonstration). Show the result at the start and at the end of the presentation. Prepare good visuals that are easy to understand and use large fonts. And most of all, practice, practice, practice.

Finally, think deeply about all of the possible objections your prospects will throw at you during the sales process. Work as many of them as possible into your proposal and presentation. If you think price will be an issue, show the prospect several reasons why price shouldn't be the deciding factor. Justify your price. Present your guarantee. If you think that schedule will be the critical factor, prepare a detailed schedule and show that you will complete the assignment ahead of the customer's required timeframe.

Operations Plan

If you are starting a new consulting business, you will want to focus on the following issues:

▶ **Facilities**: Do you want an office at home or do you want to rent office space? The trend is certainly with the former. Technology today enables many companies to be virtual (no offices, almost no overhead). The only issue is distraction. Can you concentrate at the level needed in your home?

▶ **Equipment**: I continue to be surprised by how little equipment is necessary to run your business. All I use is a laptop computer, a printer/scanner/copier, and a smartphone. That's about it.

▶ **Vendors/Suppliers**: Everyone needs help in some way to conduct their business. In my case, I have several vendors on call: my attorney, a word processor to make my reports look great, a graphic designer to help with website graphics and logos, and my accountant. Line up the vendors you need so they are ready to help when needed.

▶ **Website**: Having a website is becoming imperative for consultants these days. Websites can be used simply as a brochure, a lead generation device, or a sales portal. Most consultants use websites for lead generation, but if you're starting out, you can simply use it to present your brand, your marketing message, and your contact information.

▶ **Accounting Procedures**: Independent consultants need not be overburdened by accounting issues. The keys are time recording for billing your time, expense recording, a receivables spreadsheet to track invoicing, a payables spreadsheet to track bills to be paid, and cash management to monitor cash on hand. You might be surprised at how many businesses rely on Quicken and a qualified tax preparer!

Legal and Risk Plan

Important considerations revolving around legal issues and business risk include:

▶ Insurance
▶ Non-Disclosure Agreements
▶ Contracts
▶ Licenses
▶ Company Structure
▶ Business Risks

Starting with **insurance**, you first responsibility should be to obtain a commercial general liability insurance policy (CGL). This is the basic business insurance, and will protect you against an array of common claims, including bodily injury, property damage, personal injury, and advertising injury. Policies vary widely, so look carefully at the coverage.

Another type of insurance, called professional liability (also known as errors and omissions) will protect you against claims involving alleged negligent acts or errors that occur in the performance of your services. Many independent consultants carry this insurance. It is required if you work for many local or state governments or utilities. Some companies also require this insurance.

In addition, you may want to get insurance for your office. If you work at home, your homeowner's policy will do (but check the deductible; many homeowners' policies won't pay for the first $3,000 of any claim). If you have employees, you may need worker's compensation insurance. Check with your state for details. If you're just starting out, using independent contractors, staff from temp agencies, or other consultants like yourself may let you avoid the this expense—and it's not the only expense associated with employees!

Next, you will want to know about **non-disclosure agreements**. As a consultant, you may get an assignment from a firm that must divulge some confidential information for conducting your work. They will ask you to sign a non-disclosure agreement, also called a confidentiality agreement. This is a normal business practice—and as a consultant, part of what you're being paid for is discretion. It's bad business (and if you signed a confidentiality agreement, it's actionable) to divulge one client's corporate information to another client.

The topic of **contracts** is very important. The primary reason for contracts is to protect your practice. When you win a consulting assignment, you will either sign your contract with the client, or, more likely, you will sign the client's contract. The larger the client's company, the greater the likelihood that you'll be required to conform to their contract rules. Also, you may need a subcontract form for subconsultants or contractors you will engage.

You may be asked by a client to sign a Purchase Order in lieu of a contract. Be careful of these documents because they are legally very one-sided in favor of the client.

You can obtain professional services contract forms at LawDepot.com or other similar web sites. Then have your attorney review them for you. You should be aware of a few contract clauses (I'm not an attorney; I mention these clauses based on my experience negotiating contracts with the help of my attorney):

▶ The **compensation clause** will address your labor rates and expenses. Your labor rate should cover your costs of doing business (e.g., your overhead—cost of office space, health and liability insurance, etc.). Typically, you should ask for a mark-up on expenses of 10-15% to cover the administrative cost of spending your own money, logging it, billing for it, and paying vendors. In some cases however, a client will insist on billing expenses at cost.

▶ The **Method of Payment** clause will cover when you will be paid, and how long the client has after receiving your invoice to pay you (30 days is common). I always ask for monthly payments. This is also typical. In some cases, clients will want milestone payments. If the client wants milestone payments, first be sure you are convinced that you will get to each milestone in a reasonable timeframe. Second, make sure the definitions of the milestones are crystal clear. Third, make sure that reaching the milestones is within your control. (If a milestone requires specific actions from the client or another vendor of the client's, you have little leverage to compel them to complete on time.) In other instances, you may elect to work on a fixed cost basis (also called a lump sum).

▶ Most contracts have a **confidentiality clause** that protects the client's information or data. Make sure that the client is not restricting the use of public information.

▶ The **indemnification clause** is very important. The key here is whether this clause protects you from the client's errors and omissions. A good indemnification clause is even-handed and protects both parties against the negligence of the other.

▶ **Limit of Liability** is another clause to watch carefully. Typically, you do not want the limit of liability to exceed the value of the contract. However, this won't work for a small assignment. Just be sure that the limit is not an extreme value.

▶ **Insurance**: be sure that you can supply proof of the insurance required. If they are asking for more than you have, negotiate.

▶ Non-competition clauses can limit your options; be careful that the client does not limit or restrict your work after this assignment.

Once again, consider asking your attorney to review a client contract for you; this is especially important if you're just starting out.

In some locations, and depending on what business you're in, you will need a **license**. Check with your local government and state government.

Which **company structure** you select is also an important decision. While I have formed a number of these structures in the past, I am not an attorney. Consult with your attorney for the details. The typical choices are:

▶ **Sole Proprietorship**: The sole proprietorship is just that. There can be no employees (but you can utilize independent contractors). There are advantages and disadvantages of this structure. On the plus side, the structure is very simple and easy to implement—maybe too easy, in that it doesn't require you to keep separate records for the business. This can lead to problems in your finances. Your business-related taxes are filed as part of your personal income taxes. Losses can be deducted from your income, which helps reduce your business expenses. And, you can offset home expenses by deducting home resources consumed by the business (heating, space, electricity, communications, etc.). On the negative side of the ledger, you're required to pay federal unemployment tax (called "self-employment tax"), which is roughly 15% of your gross income—and you aren't free to collect unemployment when you're not working. Of much greater importance, your liability is unlimited; an unhappy client can go after ALL of your resources. This problem can be partially alleviated through professional liability insurance.

▶ **Partnership**: A partnership is similar to that of a sole proprietorship in some respects. A partnership can have two or more employees, so you have a greater talent pool. The partners share the profits. However, disagreements may occur with regard to how the profits should be distributed. Your liability is still unlimited, unless you opt for a Limited Partnership, where the partners' liability is equal to their investment in the firm. Limited Partnerships must have a license. I would be very careful of partnerships. Two "CEOs" typically does not work in the long run.

▶ **Limited Liability Company**: The limited liability company has some distinct advantages over the previous two structures for some applications. The liability exposure is limited to the resources contained in the firm. In addition, there are a number of tax benefits. Capital is easier to attract because of the liability issue. However, LLCs are subject to state and federal regulations. As such, licensing fees can be significant. Income and dividends are not double taxed. Overall, I like the LLC structure for a firm that may be exposed to some liabilities. It is the simplest structure that does provide liability protection.

▶ **S Corporation**: The S corporation is an alternative to the LLC. Both provide liability protection. The S corporation provides a tax benefit on the employment tax. An LLC is taxed on total income, while S corporations are taxed only the net income (minus salaries). The S corporation is considered to have beneficial tax advantages in many states. However, the S corporation has many more federal filing requirements. Finally, in an S corporation, profits must be distributed in accord with the stock ownership. This is a key restriction.

▶ **C Corporation**: The C corporation is the standard corporate structure. There are fewer restrictions on shareholders, and better tax shelters.

Consult your CPA or attorney to decide on the best structure for you.

Finally, let's briefly address **business risks**. From my personal experience, here are a few risks that you will want to manage properly or avoid:

▶ **Competition**: Always be aware of your competition. Are you differentiating yourself from them? We include this issue as a risk because a competitor in your client firm may try to replace you. Always be alert.

▶ **Receivable Days**: Watch your receivables and call clients who are not paying on time. If you are a small firm that cannot operate if bills are not paid promptly, communicate that. Many clients have policies that will pay small vendors quickly. Ask about them.

▶ **Client Disputes**: Respond to client complaints quickly before they begin to negatively affect your relationship. Go the extra mile to satisfy an unhappy client. Try to include a clause in your contract that says you will be paid for all work NOT in dispute. This will prevent the client from holding up all payments until a specific dispute is settled.

▶ **Work Overload**: Don't work too much overtime without taking some time off to recharge the batteries. You should take small breaks daily, and plan time off now and then. You will find that a bit of down time will help you create new ideas.

Financial Plan

If you're not into planning, *at least do your financial plan.* This is, by far, the most important part of your business plan! If you are just starting out, you need to carefully plan your expenses and cash flow. If you need to raise money for your new business venture, a number of alternatives are available.

You may need money to start your practice or service business. One source of funds, of course, is you. That should be your first choice, rather than going into debt. However, if you need to tap a funding source, there are a number of alternatives. One alternative I have accessed several times is the Line of Credit. You can arrange a Line of Credit

Financial Plan
Pro-forma Income Statement

Net Sales	$80,000	
Cost of Sales		$20,000
Gross Profit		60,000
Operating Expenses		
Selling, G&A		15,000
Depreciation		-
Operating Income	$45,000	
Other Income		
Interest Income		1,000
Interest Expense		(3,000)
Income before Taxes		43,000
Income Tax Expense		12,000
Net Income		31,000

with most any bank. The requirements are not rigid. However, the interest rate will be high (these days, around 10%). One advantage is that you only borrow the money you need. You don't get a lump sum like a personal loan. So, if you think that you can repay the loan within a reasonable amount of time, this is a good choice. Non-collateralized Lines of Credit are available up to $50,000-$100,000.

If you are working for someone else, sweat equity might be an answer. In this case, you work for a share of the company. Friends and family are great sources of funds because the interest rate typically will be lower, and the restrictions will be less. Some credit cards allow cash disbursement. However, the withdrawal limits are quite low.

Personal loans can be obtained from a variety of sources, such as credit unions or banks. You may need to be employed to be eligible. Microloans are small business loans, typically around $5,000-$10,000, but can go as high as $25,000. A number of entities offer these loans. However, there are restrictions that involve your credit rating, and your ability to meet the payments. Check www.microloan.com. A Small Business Administration loan is also possible. Check www.sba.gov.

An important aspect of financial planning is the pro forma income statement. You create this statement to determine how much funding you will need, and for how many months your funding will take you. This pro forma statement is stationary in time. You will need to create one that looks at the next twelve months or more so you can see the impact of time on your cash on hand.

Start by estimating your revenues, or sales. Then calculate your cost of sales, which includes the expenses involved in your service, such as travel expenses, that would be billed directly to clients. Then estimate your operating expenses. This would include your marketing expenses, rent, insurance, electricity, phone, Internet, payments for loans, payments for equipment such as computers, and so on. Add in any other income, such as interest income, or interest expense from loans. Finally, estimate your tax liability, and compute your profit. Once again, you need to do this by month for at least a year to get a reasonable picture of your ability to stay afloat until your business at least achieves breakeven.

Finally, recordkeeping in the financial area is very important. Set up spreadsheets, or use software packages like Quicken or QuickBooks to track the following:

▶ **Checking Account Balance**: keeping up with your checking account keeps your business expenses and profits clearer; this is a great benefit for you and your tax preparer.

▶ **Accounts Receivable**: It is critical that you collect fees owed you in a timely fashion. Inform the client when you send an invoice. Follow up every two weeks. If it appears that the client is delaying payment, determine if there is a problem with your invoice. Be very careful about stopping work. In my experience, that only exacerbates the problem. In addition, check your contract and talk to your attorney.

▶ **Accounts Payable**: keep your bills up to date so you don't hurt your suppliers. Be aware that you may need to pay suppliers before you get paid by the client.

Keeping track of the above in a program like Quickbooks will allow you to create Profit & Loss Statements (also called the Income Statement), which provide a measure of the profitability of the business by comparing expenses with revenues; accounts receivable reports, which display all of your open invoices and show which clients may be behind in payments; and many other reports you'll find useful.

Keep track of your assets, especially your accounts receivable, cash, and inventory (if applicable). Watch your operating expenses and administrative and marketing expenses. This is where most consultants go awry.

Billing for Your Services

There are many ways to bill for your services. Let's look at the most common ones:

▶ **Time and Materials**, or T&M, is the most common billing method. You simply bill the client for services by the hour, using an agreed upon hourly rate. You also bill expenses to the client. There are two ways to bill for expenses. First, you bill at cost. Or, you add a mark-up to pay for processing costs and insurance costs. Typical markups are 5% to 15%. If you engage a sub-consultant, you can usually add a mark-up to cover administrative costs of managing the sub-consultant.

▶ **Firm Fixed Price/Lump Sum**: Another popular pricing method is firm fixed price or lump sum (they mean the same thing). In this method, you will agree to perform the scope of work for a set price. In most instances, you should add a contingency (5-10%) to account for unanticipated work. *Be very careful with this method if the scope is not well defined.*

▶ **Not-to-Exceed** without authorization: This method can be viewed as a compromise between the first two methods. Not-to-Exceed provides some flexibility on the price. The key, however, is to tell the client well in advance if you think you will exceed the budget.

▶ **Cost Plus Performance Fee**: In this method, you will perform the work at cost, then add an agreed upon fee. The fee can be a percentage of the cost (this is favorable to the consultant), or a fixed fee (favorable to the client).

▶ **Cost Plus Fixed Fee** with guaranteed maximum: Here, we perform the work at cost, then add a fixed fee. However, there is a maximum or cap that cannot be breached. This provides protection to the client in the case of excessive overruns. The consultant holds most of the risk.

▶ **Value-based Pricing**: In this situation, you bundle your services into a package, and assign a value based upon the perceived value. This value is typically a function of the trust you have earned, how unique your service is (e.g., is it available from other consultants?), and the value the client attaches to the service (related to the expected results, such as speed, lower cost, or higher revenues). Your remuneration under this scenario would exceed your fee based upon your cost-basis (e.g., the number of hours expended times your hourly rate).

▶ **Performance-based Pricing:** In this situation, you agree to be paid based upon the results, or profits, you achieve. Marketing consultants often use this model. For example, a marketing consultant sees an opportunity to improve business profits by enhancing the marketing process. The consultant may suggest a new market channel, or the use of Internet marketing techniques. The consultant would receive no fee until and unless the business's profit is increased as a result of the new technique. Typical fees in these situations range up to 50% of the business's increased profit. As you can see, this could be very lucrative. Of course, the consultant must be rather sure that he can achieve the results promised. In addition, be sure a good contract is in place.

All of these methods are useful in certain situations. Some are more favorable to consultants, such as time and materials and lump sum. When determining a pricing or fee strategy, always be aware of scope uncertainty.

Billing Rate

When deciding on a billing rate, four criteria come into play: operational expenses, your experience, your expertise, and the market rate. Let's take a brief look at each factor:

▶ **Operational Expenses:** Clearly, you will need sufficient funds to cover your firm's expenses and provide some profit to live on. You need to determine a billing rate that will accomplish this.

▶ **Your Experience**: More experience, typically measured in years, leads to a higher billing rate. You have to get some actual rate data for your field to determine the specific relationship between rate and experience.

▶ **Your Expertise**: Your rate also is a function of your expertise, including your education.

▶ **Market Rate**: Finally, there is a market rate for virtually every position. You may be able to find the results of a salary survey that will identify an approximate market rate.

In actuality, all of these factors come into play. For technical professional positions, typical billing rates at the entry level are $40-$70/hour. Ten years of experience may bring $100-$150/hour, and twenty years $150-$250/hour.

Note that if you are a sole proprietor, you should have a competitive advantage versus a consulting firm pricing the same service. Consulting firms will have a higher markup to cover offices, equipment, training, administrative expenses, tax issues, and so on.

OK, it's time that you completed the last section of the Success Roadmap, Section 14 – The Business Plan. By this time, I trust that you have completed many of the business planning tasks listed at the start of this chapter. As a result, it should be easy to finish your Business Plan, and get that shingle out!

7. Your Roadmap to Success

The purpose of this chapter is to create your Roadmap to Success. The roadmap is intended to be a specific and detailed blueprint that will get you off to a rapid start in your business, or off to an effective improvement plan if you are in business.

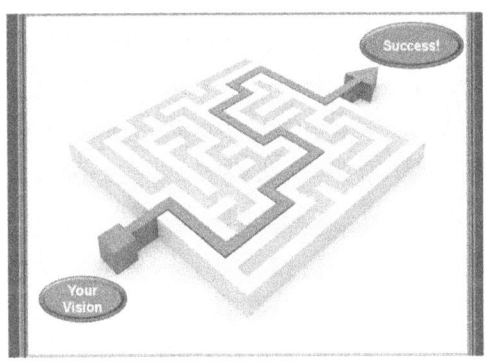

Get a notebook that you can use to complete your roadmap. There are fourteen exercises that will be entered into the notebook. I recommend a 3-ring binder with tab inserts so you can add paper as needed.

You may be tempted to use your computer rather than writing on paper. Even if you are in the habit of using a computer for most of your work, I strongly recommend that you at least try starting your roadmap on paper. Several studies have been performed that suggest writing longhand engages a different part of our brains and brings key information to the forefront of the brain's filters.

Take the time needed to complete this roadmap. As I said at the outset, actually implementing what you have read about is a necessity if you want to learn this material. In addition, the roadmap exercises provide a great way to review the material we covered. That is another way to increase retention.

Creating your Roadmap for Success comprises the following tasks:

1. Define Your Business Objective

2. Reverse Engineer the Objective

3. Set Your Goals

4. Specify Your Action Items

5. Mind Your Mindset!

6. What is Your Offering

7. Prepare Your Marketing Plan

8. Develop Your Sales Plan

9. Develop Your Proposal Template

10. Develop Your Problem Assessment Technique

11. How Will You Select the Best Solution?

12. What is Your Client Relationship Plan?

13. Prepare Your Project Management Plan

14. Prepare Your Business Plan & Get Started!

OK, so get out your notebook, and let's get started!

1. Define Your Business Objective

The first step towards creating your Roadmap to Success is to define your business objective. Let's start with a definition of the term "objective". Your business objective must be specific, realistic, measurable, and time-delineated.

In other words, describe what you want your business to look like in two-to-three years. How many employees do you need at that time? What revenue will support those employees? How many clients do you need to support that revenue? How will you improve your service during this period?

As an example, a solar firm I helped found had the following business objective at the outset: "Develop ten utility-scale ground-mount solar projects in California and sell them to companies that will build and own these projects within 3 years. Prefer three or four clients with multiple projects each. Minimize the number of full-time employees to keep expenses low."

Now it is time for you to write your business objective. Go to your Roadmap for Success notebook and enter your objectives. Remember: the only wrong way to do this is to *not* do it. You will likely refine almost every step of your roadmap during the course of reading this book and of enrolling partners, clients, and champions in your business goals.

2. Reverse Engineer the Objective

The next step consists of reverse engineering the objective. That is, identify the steps needed to take you from the objective backwards (in reverse time) to the present. We go back in time because it is usually easier to start from the end point. The idea is to generally describe what must be accomplished in Year 3 (if that was your completion year), then to Year 2, and Year 1. It is best to describe what must be done by quarter or half-year. This is the beginning of your roadmap. Work at the Interstate highway level, not the street level.

Carrying our solar business example further, recall that the endpoint was to sell ten projects at the conclusion of Year 3. To meet the objective, we would need to receive all of our milestone (i.e., progress) payments (several per project) by the end of Year 3. Or, we would need to receive half of the payments during the first part of Year 3. In Year 2, we must prepare the projects for sale (e.g., perform surveys, environmental work, public relations, legal work, and so on). In Year 1, we must identify enough potential sites to ensure ten projects in Years 2 and 3. This is a rough outline of accomplishments that must occur.

Now try to reverse engineer your objective. Think about what needs to be accomplished from achievement of your objective backwards to the present. Do your reverse engineering in your Roadmap to Success notebook.

3. Set Your Goals

The next step is to develop a set of business goals that must be met to achieve your objective. Once again, start at the objective, and work back in time. Use the work you did in the last step as a guide. Basically, you are adding more detail and becoming more specific. For example, move from the Interstate to state and county roads.

Goals should be developed with timeframes of a month, for example, or, at most, by quarter, when the objective is 2 or 3 years off. Specifically, what will you accomplish in each month or quarter? Include the completion date and the purpose of each goal.

Using our solar project example once more, let's look at goals for Year 1. The objective of Year 1 is to identify enough potential project sites that subsequent work in

---

"The major reason for setting a goal is what it makes of you to accomplish it. What it makes of you will always be of far greater value than what you get."
Jim Rohn

Years 2 and 3 will yield at least the ten projects required. The following goals pertained to Year 1: a) Inspect at least six California counties to ensure that sufficient project sites could be identified; b) Identify approximately 200 potential project sites within the six counties to ensure that ten fully vetted project sites can be found; c) Find 25 candidate project sites that will pass the application of stringent criteria to identify sites that are both permittable and economically feasible.

As a review, setting goals, and reading those goals often, creates a "mental reality" in your subconscious brain. This "reality" becomes the aim of your subconscious mind, and it will work to create a corresponding physical reality, that is, a completed goal.

Now, develop your goals. Give yourself specific targets that need to be met in order to achieve your business objective. Go to your Roadmap to Success notebook and enter your business goals.

4. Specify Your Action Items

Next, you need to convert your goals, or targets, to more specific *actions*. In other words, dig deeper into what must be accomplished, and express exactly what must be done to reach your business objective. Now you are moving from just identifying the Interstate highway or state/county highway to specifying the local streets that will get you to your destination.

OK, let's use our solar project example for the last time! Now we need to convert the goals into specific actions. For example, we said in the previous section that ten projects must be identified from the 25 candidate sites. The actions that must be taken to reach this target are: a) determine if the candidate sites can be permitted (e.g., review biological data, hydrological data, cultural data to see if there are insurmountable constraints), b) determine if the candidate sites can be built with reasonable site development costs (e.g., close to electric transmission lines, flat or almost flat topography, close to established roads, good subsurface conditions with no hazards), and c) few to no residents or commercial establishments adjacent to the site.

You should be able to see the difference in detail between this section and prior sections. These "action items" are very specific, and can be implemented in a straightforward manner.

Now, once again, it is time for you to list specific actions that are needed to reach your business objective. Enter your specific actions in your Roadmap to Success notebook.

5. Mind Your Mindset

Remember the Consultant's Cycle of Success I introduced in Chapter 1? It contained the seven essential behaviors that I saw in my career that invariably lead to success in consulting: vision, goal setting, enthusiasm, focus, creativity, teamship, and mastery. Adhering to these behaviors helps establish the proper "success mindset"—and if you're feeling uncertain about how well you're answering the questions in this chapter, I recommend taking a look at the details of each behavior in Chapter 1. I believe they will rekindle any inspiration you may have lost as you dived into the details of your roadmap, and remind you that each step you're taking here is in order to fulfill your "big picture" desires and goals.

Another way to look at mindset is to consider actions that you can take that will strengthen your growth mindset. Remember, the stronger your mindset, the more effective you will be, and the faster you will see the results you desire.

Over the years, I've run across six actions that will support your mindset. Let's take a quick look at each.

> "My greatest challenge has been to change the mindset of people. Mindsets play strange tricks on us. We see things the way our minds have instructed our eyes to see."
>
> *Mohammad Yunus*

In no particular order, the first is **visualization**. Many athletes create mental pictures of themselves winning a race. Similarly, you can create a mental image of you achieving a goal. Use props that reinforce your thoughts. For example, if you want a corvette, buy a small model and keep it on your desk, where you can see it. Visualization helps program your subconscious mind by creating a "mental reality" that will be used by your mind to manifest what you want. When you visualize your vision and goals, you create a mental picture of your future in your subconscious. This is a powerful tool.

The second action is **affirmations**. Most people frown on this because they think it is foolish. However, many of the most successful people in history swear by them. One of the most famous affirmations is "Every day, in every way, I'm getting better and better". W. Clement Stone always woke up and exclaimed, "I feel terrific!" Saying these simple though powerful statements each day makes strong impressions on your subconscious brain. Positive affirmations will keep you positive. Note that affirmations, if used daily, help program your mind through repetition.

> "Having Dr. W. Edwards Deming as a mentor was the single most influential event in my consulting career."
>
> Dan Predpall

Third, we can use a **mentor**. Mentors provide positive support and supplemental direction when you need it. Many of the most successful executives today have mentors. Mentors, or coaches, have been successful in their businesses. Therefore, they provide new reference points, or "success environments" for you. You start to believe that you, too, can be successful.

Fourth, expand your **expertise**. The more knowledge and skills you have, the confident you get. Napoleon Hill called this "accurate knowledge". Learning also creates new references and new beliefs, and is crucial is developing a better mindset.

Fifth is taking **action**. It always feels good when you get out there and do something. This also improves your mindset. Napoleon Hill very correctly stated that if you don't take action, your confidence will atrophy. Johann Goethe's quote hits home: "Knowing is not enough; we must apply. Willing is not enough; we must do."

Action results from **intention**, a source of energy that says you are willing to do whatever it takes to accomplish your goals. Intention connects your mental picture of the future with real accomplishment. As stated by the Upanishads, intention is the source of creation and manifestation.

Sixth, we must get **results**. Nothing improves the mindset more than getting the results we need. The results don't have to be great. When you create your goals, break them down into sub-goals that can be completed in a week or two. This will provide regular positive reinforcement.

As you get the results you want, keep taking your "success vitamins": more learning, more goal setting, more visualization, and more new reference points provided by your mentors.

Now get out there and write down three things you will do to improve your mindset! Enter your mindset actions in your Roadmap to Success notebook.

6. What is Your Offering?

Most consultants don't think deeply enough about their service or product offering. After all, it is just an offering. Hold on. It does not matter what your offering is if you don't make it congruent with your prospects' needs and wants. The more you think about your offering, the more ways you will discover to explain your product to your customer, and your explanation will be more concise, and, therefore, easier for them to understand. Got it?

In Chapter 2, I offered a list of ten questions about your offer and asked if you could answer them. If you jotted down notes, then it's time to refine and write down the answers in your Roadmap to Success notebook. I'm giving you the same questions again below, but worded a little differently. Think very carefully about these basic questions regarding your offering:

1. What is it called? What does this name mean? Do you have a logo?

2. What is your offering, in one or two short sentences.

3. What does it do, in a couple short sentences.

4. How does it do this, in two short sentences.

5. What two major benefits are derived from this offering by the customer?

6. How is it different from competitors' offerings?

7. What is this offering worth to the customer, in dollar terms?

8. What is the cost of this offering, and what is your price for the offering?

9. What guarantees are you able to give for your offering's success?

Now, let's focus on your potential customers. Think very carefully about the prospect's needs, and answer these questions:

▶ What is the prospect's key problem?
▶ What is the underlying problem?
▶ What is the cause of the problem?
▶ What are the symptoms of the problem?
▶ What is your solution to the problem?

Remember to look at both emotional and rational issues. Some causes might be overwhelm, poor marketing, insufficient profit, poor revenue stream, lack of confidence, poor performance, or lack of creative ideas. Differentiate between root causes and symptoms. Describe your offering in your Roadmap to Success notebook.

Okay. You have completed steps 1 through 6, so now it's time to go back up to Chapter 3 and enjoy a little more reading. We'll work on sections 7 through 14 soon.

7. Prepare Your Marketing Plan

Now we are ready to add marketing your service to your roadmap. You have to conduct three tasks: describe your service and package it attractively, define who your prospects are, and select your marketing channels.

First, describe your service in a way that your clients will want, not what you want. Package the service smartly and professionally. Next, define your prospects. Who will be your best clients? Do the required market research so you have confidence answering this question.

> "By failing to prepare, you are preparing to fail."
>
> Benjamin Franklin

Third, select the marketing channels that will maximize your return on marketing effort. The usual suspects are direct marketing, Internet marketing, conference attendance, publishing articles/books, advertising, and affiliates or alliance partners. Choose the best one for you, and then gradually add more channels.

For example, suppose you wanted to sell vintage women's clothing online. Start by describing your service. What type of clothing will you specialize? What era will you concentrate on? What is the condition of your clothing? Next, define who your prospects or customers will be. Women, I am sure, but of what age group? Third, select the marketing channels. In this case, you might select either your own website (the most challenging way to start an online business), or, better, open a store on Etsy. com. If you have more than one type of clothing, or if certain clothing may attract different age groups, open a second store. Once they are going, open a store on eBay. Set up a Facebook page for your business. Finally, create your own website.

Now it's your turn. What is your marketing plan? Enter your Marketing Plan in your Roadmap to Success notebook.

8. Prepare Your Sales Plan

Next, it is time to develop your sales plan. You have initiated your marketing, and now you need to decide how to sell your service to prospects who indicate an interest in your service. Assume that your marketing has turned up a few potentially attractive prospects.

The next step is to gather some intelligence to learn about them. What types of services are they buying? Who are they buying from? Once you understand them based upon your intelligence, develop a contact plan. How will you meet the prospect? Can you get a referral? Make a cold call? See the prospect at a meeting or conference? Use email to get his/her attention, and then propose a meeting?

Let's suppose you have just moved to a new area, and your expertise is a health & safety trainer. How do you prepare your sales plan? Your marketing plan has told you that the possible clients include health & safety professionals in pharmaceutical and utility companies nearby. Your contact plan should include making personal calls on the firms in your area. If the cold call approach is uncomfortable, try meeting employees at these firms. They probably show up at local business meetings, such as the Board of Trade, Chamber of Commerce,

Economic Development Corporation, or similar organization. Then just ask the contact for a referral to the health & safety department. Another approach is to look at the websites for these firms. They may show contact information.

Next, develop your "stadium pitch", or 30-second concise description of your service and its benefits. Develop a free gift that you can provide to new contacts (a free report, conference paper you might have presented, etc.). Prepare a template for a sales letter. Remember to use psychological triggers!

OK, now it is time for you to prepare a sales plan. Remember (or review) the section in Chapter 5 entitled, "What Clients Want From You". Your marketing plan should answer as many of those questions as it can, and your plan should *definitely* represent your brand. Enter your plan, including your stadium pitch and sales letter template into your Roadmap to Success notebook.

9. Develop Your Proposal Template

Hopefully, your marketing and sales efforts will bear fruit. You need to be prepared to write a proposal, or present a proposal, to win the job. If you are lucky, there will be no competition (i.e., sole source opportunity). However, in most cases, you will compete against others.

First, develop an attractive proposal format (logo, graphics, pictures, etc. to enhance readability).

Second, develop an outline (usually an introduction, where you can sell, followed by a problem statement to show you understand the problem, an approach (high-level process statement), methodology (how you will perform the work), your biographical sketch, your experience, and cost/schedule.

Third, develop your key benefits (how your service is different from your competitor's) and features. Benefits are why the customer will want your service. Features are descriptors, like where your office is located, or how many employees you have).

The most important part of a proposal is the discussion of benefits. This is where "the rubber meets the road". The best kinds of benefits are those that represent the wants of the decision-makers, as opposed to the needs of the company itself. In other words, see if you can learn what drives the decision-makers. This could be security, notoriety, recognition, etc.

The needs of the company also provide sources of benefits. For example, their annual plan will include a number of projects that must be completed. This provides opportunities for consultants. In addition, benefits can include opportunities to save money, save time, or save work.

If your service is complex, you will want to use a formal proposal structure that contains the sections mentioned above. However, if the service is not complex, use a letter proposal format. In this instance, the proposal might be two or three pages. Always begin the letter with a sales pitch, describe how your service will help the client, and show what your service does. Then describe your experience, and better yet, include one or more testimonials to your work.

Work on your template. The template contains the material that will be in each proposal. Add some notes in your

Success Roadmap Notebook regarding your proposal template (e.g., some of your best persuasive writing).

10. Develop Your Problem Assessment Technique

In this section, we address your service. It is vital that you are able to describe your service in detail, and in a way that the client can understand it, and see the benefits of using your service.

The first step in describing your service, try to develop a framework or model, of your service. The purpose of the framework is to show how the service works. Also, it will show the client that you understand the service and that you likely have provided this service in the past (because you have a "template" or framework). This framework will be inserted into the Approach section of your proposal document.

Second, describe a process by which you will perform the service. What is the step-by-step procedure that you will apply? This process will become the basis for your Methodology section of your proposal.

Third, try to create a few interesting graphics that can be used to show the framework or process. The adage "a picture is worth a thousand words" applies here.

Fourth, if your service is, in many respects, similar to services offered by your competitors, you must find a way to differentiate your service from the others. One way to do this is to carry out the service in a different series of steps. Another is to demonstrate that your service is more effective, or less in cost, than others in the marketplace. Or, you can package the service creatively.

Now describe your service by applying the concepts above. Enter your problem assessment technique in your Success Roadmap Notebook.

11. How will You Select the Best Solution?

Most of you, while performing your service, will need to justify selecting one particular solution to a problem. On other words, many services involve finding a solution that best fits the situation. This applies even to the most basic of services.

For example, a plumber is called to a home to assess a water leak in the basement. There are likely multiple ways to fix the leak, from a quick (maybe a patch) fix, to a more costly, but more effective fix (replace the pipe in question). How does the plumber decide which fix is appropriate? Hopefully, he considers the long-term effectiveness of the fix, and the cost. Perhaps he offers two options for to consider.

It is important that you develop a clear rationale for deciding which solution should be selected. Many decisions are based on cost. Others are based on time elapsed. Still others might be chosen based on quality. In some cases, however, the decision will involve multiple objectives (such as cost and time).

For example, when selecting the best sites for industrial applications, such as power facilities, decisions rest on several variables, including site development cost, public acceptability, environmental impacts, and impacts on people. The choice is made using decision analysis techniques.

Mentioning this decision process to clients is a significant benefit.

If your service involves a choice of alternative solutions, you should adopt a decision process. This will become part of your service description. It will be a good differentiator. And, it will instill confidence of the client in your ability to make the correct decision on their behalf.

Describe your decision technique or process in your Success Roadmap Notebook.

12. What is Your Client Relationship Plan?

Your roadmap should include a plan for building solid client relationships. Most consultants make their money on repeat business, not new clients. What should you do to create great client relationships?

One of the most important "to do's" is to be accessible 24/7. That doesn't mean stay awake all night, but it does mean checking your email when you awake every morning and just before you retire at night, and leave your cell phone on as much as possible during the day and evening.

When communicating with the client, always offer your help, even if the subject is a personal one. The client will begin to feel that you are available and willing. You will get the call when he does need help.

Be cognizant of the "Client Need Formula". If you are in frequent contact with your prospector client when the formula is satisfied, you will be in the right position. The formula is Opportunity = Need x Importance x Urgency. If the prospect or client has a need, it is an important one (e.g., his boss wants it), and it is urgent, you have a good opportunity.

When you meet the client in person, establish a rapport by asking about his family, or some aspect of his background.

If it is the first meeting in his office, look at the pictures on the wall, and ask about one of them. Try to find common ground.

Always try to offer your prospect or client fresh ideas or free services that demonstrate your commitment, and expertise. This positions you as the expert, not the salesman.

How will you build a relationship with your prospect or client? Enter your client Relationship Plan in your Success Roadmap Notebook.

13. Prepare Your Project Management Plan

OK, now you have won a project, or assignment. How do you manage this assignment successfully? Good project management will impress the client and tell him that you are in control.

You should prepare a brief Project Management Plan that provides a checklist for solid project success.

Here is an outline of a basic Project Management Plan:

1.0   Client Contact Information

2.0   Scope of Work & Deliverables

3.0   Project Budget Tracking

4.0   Project Schedule Tracking

5.0   Communication Protocol

6.0   Billing & Invoicing Procedures

The client contact information is straightforward. The work scope should be detailed, and include specifics on what the deliverable should contain. The budget tracking section should include a spreadsheet that will be used to summarize expenditures by month and remaining budget, along with a notes column to indicate any potential or real budget problems. For example, is there any scope creep?

The project schedule tracking section should contain a Gantt chart that shows project schedule status. Check to see if expenditures are tracking the schedule progress (i.e., are you spending money too fast?).

The communication protocol section should indicate how and how frequently you should communicate with your client. What methods will you use (that the client has requested), such as email, phone, website, progress reporting, face-to-face meetings, etc. Remember, you want to favor more in-person meetings, which build relationships.

Develop a reliable procedure to memorialize your labor and expenses with a clear timesheet and expense report template (time and expenses can be recorded on the same form). Break a job into several separate tasks if needed, to enhance work tracking and billing. You want the record to be clear, so the client can see what you are doing. Finally, create a simple invoice form for billing the client on a monthly basis.

So, now it is your turn. Create your Project Management Plan, along with a timesheet, expense report form, and invoice template.

Now enter your Project Management Plan in your Success Notebook. This plan can be brief. However, address each topic listed above that is applicable to your business.

14. Prepare Your Business Plan

The last task you need to do before "hanging your shingle" is the Business Plan. This is where "the rubber meets the road". I decided to insert another Jim Rohn quote here. When you read it the first time, it may not seem applicable to the topic of this section. However, I think it has immense relevance. Read it again. It reveals the *real* reason why we need to plan for everything.

Here are the contents of the Business Plan:

1.0   Business Goals

2.0   Service Description

3.0   Marketing & Sales Plan

4.0   Management Plan

5.0   Financial Plan

6.0   Legal Plan

7.0   Risk Management Plan

> *"If you don't design your own life plan, chance are you'll fall into someone else's plan. And guess what they have planned for you? Not much."*
>
> *Jim Rohn*

We have already covered your Business Goals, Service Description, Marketing & Sales Plan, and Management Plan. Now let's briefly discuss your Financial Plan, Legal Plan, and Risk Management Plan.

The Financial Plan addresses three subjects: company structure, raising start-up funds, and forecasting your cash flow. For purposes of the roadmap, it is assumed that you have settled on a company structure. The key issue is whether you have sufficient funds to conduct your work for the time needed to build an income.

You must create a cash flow forecast, where you start with the funds available, and estimate expenses for the first months of the enterprise. If you need more cash, there are a number of potential sources, including friends and family, personal loans, lines-of-credit, and SBA loans. Most people who are starting out will work part-time and consult part-time until they develop a sufficient and reliable revenue stream.

With regard to legal issues, you don't need much legal support to get started. The key legal support you need are a) a services contract that can be obtained online or through your attorney, b) an attorney who can review client contracts when needed (one option is to join Pre-Paid Legal for this help), and c) get a commercial general liability insurance policy. Most clients will require this insurance.

In some cases, a firm may require Professional Liability insurance. This is quite expensive, so if the client requires it, see if they are willing to pay for it.

With regard to risk management, the most important issue is getting paid. Watch your "receivable days" carefully. Build a relationship with the Client's Accounts Payable section. This will greatly help you get paid on time.

OK, spend some time outlining your Financial Plan, and get the legal support you need. Place a summary of your Business Plan in your Success Roadmap Notebook.

Time to FLY

Now you need to TAKE ACTION! Don't come up with excuses like "I am not a real expert", or "I need to be perfect before I begin".

You have the roadmap. Start your journey to success! Move up to a higher level of success!

Keep these quotes in mind:

> *"Action is the foundational key to all success."*
> Pablo Picasso

> *"Create a definite plan for carrying out your desire, and begin at once, ready or not."*
> Napoleon Hill

> *"Even if you're on the right track, you'll get run over if you just sit there."*
> Will Rogers

Here's my favorite saying for getting unstuck (this one is profound):

> *"If things didn't go my way today, there are only two reasons why:*
>
> 1. *I didn't give it the time needed, or*
>
> 2. *I didn't know enough."*
>
> Dan Predpall

Remember, we at Successful Consultant Training are here to support you!

Post your questions and comments on our Facebook page: www.facebook.com/successfulconsultanttraining

We would love to hear from you. Or, email us at:

info@successfulconsultanttraining.com

If you enjoyed learning the material in this book, you may be interested in our basic Consulting Course DVD Set. You get 5 DVDs with 115 lessons covering all of the topics we addressed in this book, and much more. We've included many examples and case histories, and we drill deeper into many topics, such as marketing and sales and problem solving.

In addition, we will be offering online webinars on many of the topics discussed here. See our website for details.

Inquire at info@successfulconsultanttraining.com or go to our website at: www.successfulconsultanttraining.com/store.

We also publish a monthly newsletter loaded with great tips and techniques. Sign up for a free subscription at the same locations mentioned above.

About the Author

Dan Predpall, P.E. **Founder and President of Successful Consultant Training**

Founder and President

- ▶ B.S. Physics and Electrical Engineering, Stevens Institute of Technology

- ▶ M.S. Physical Oceanography, Long Island University

- ▶ MBA Quantitative Analysis, New York University

- ▶ Advisor/Mentor: Dr. Edwards Deming

- ▶ Over 35 years of experience in consulting

▶ Leading expert on site selection for industrial facilities

▶ Senior executive of a multi-billion dollar consulting-engineering firm

▶ Founded several small development firms and sole proprietorships

One of the most important things that ever happened to me began, improbably, in a statistics class. The course was taught by W. Edwards Deming, one of the most remarkable men of the 20th century. When he became my mentor he was one of the most influential and successful consultants in the world, having, among many triumphs, dramatically revolutionized the manufacturing cultures in both Japan and America. What I learned from him changed the direction of my life. His kindness, generosity, and the thousands of lives he helped transform for the better continue to inspire me. After 35 years of consulting, I want share what I've learned, to give back by making a positive difference in the lives and careers of as many people as I possibly can.

One of the principles Dr. Deming emphasized over and over is the importance of a commitment to "continuous learning." I say it like this: "continuous learning is the best path to prosperity." I've spent decades learning the best consulting practices, and I'm ready, willing and able to teach them to others. One thing I've loved about consulting is that the learning never stops. Consulting has provided me with success, flexibility, freedom, and self-respect. If you're thinking about consulting or you're already consulting and want to learn how to be better at it, I can help you get where you want to go.

I've created my own companies and worked for some of the biggest and most successful consulting companies in the world. I've traveled the world helping clients make intelligent, informed choices and undertake good and important projects. I've pursued the higher calling of consulting and improved people's lives. I'm particularly proud of my work with Pacific Valley LLC, a developer of distributed solar energy facilities; Opti-Site International, a firm specializing in power plant siting for the power industry; and Community Assets Consulting, which consults about corporate responsibility, sustainability, and environmental fund development. I've contributed to the development of a lot of megawatts of solar-powered electricity at home and around the world.

I founded Successful Consulting Training to teach others how to start a lucrative career as an independent consultant, create a better lifestyle, and reap the rewards from helping other people improve their lives and their businesses.

An e-Learning Company

INDEX

www.ingramcontent.com/pod-product-compliance
Lightning Source LLC
Chambersburg PA
CBHW051517170526
45165CB00002B/502